FAMILIA

ULSTER GENEALOGICAL REVIEW

Ulster
Genealogical
& Historical
Guild

NUMBER 21

2005

THE MEMBERSHIP ASSOCIATION OF
ULSTER HISTORICAL FOUNDATION

FRONT COVER PAINTING
The Departure of O'Neill out of Ireland
by Thomas Ryan, 1958
Reproduced by kind permission of the artist

Published 2005
by Ulster Historical Foundation
12 College Square East, Belfast, BT1 6DD
www.ancestryireland.com
www.booksireland.org.uk

ISBN 13: 978-1-903688-58-8
ISBN 10: 1-903688-58-2

Printed by ColourBooks Ltd
Design and production, Dunbar Design

CONTENTS

FAMILIA

EDITORIAL

The image on the cover of this, the twenty-first edition of *Familia*, is 'The departure of O'Neill out of Ireland' by Thomas Ryan. It represents one of the most iconic events in an epoch, the start of the seventeenth century, which saw changes introduced that would continue to have implications for Irish society at home and abroad for the next four centuries. In terms of migration to and from Ulster, it marked the movement abroad, principally to Europe, of the leaders of the great Irish families and with it the loss of control and, even more importantly, land. Much of this land was in due course taken up by those who had been awarded land in the official plantation of Ulster that had been inaugurated by James I. The four-hundredth anniversary of this 'Flight of the Earls' in September 1607 will be commemorated over the next two years, an appropriate opportunity to re-consider seventeenth-century migration to and from Ulster, building on the excellent work in this field evident in the published research of Raymond Gillespie and my colleague in the Centre for Migration Studies at the Ulster American Folk Park, Paddy Fitzgerald.

Familia has played a modest role in informing the reconsideration that has been taking shape over the last twenty years of our understanding of the nature, even the extent, of emigration from Ireland in the eighteenth century. Our efforts in that direction are sustained in this edition by contributions from Kenneth Keller and Peter Gilmore who describe, respectively, the medical heritage that was transported with the migrants and merged with that of other ethnic groupings, and the extent to which the chain migration process, an issue that has featured in *Familia* in recent times, was fuelled by the provision made in the wills of settled immigrants for kith and kin still in Ireland.

The theme of land is one that is of common interest to historians and genealogical researchers alike, and both will find enormous benefit in the article by Anne Casement on the Londonderry family estates. The family's lands in counties Donegal, Londonderry, Down and Antrim constituted one of the largest landed estates in Ulster and this study raises a number of issues about their management, particularly in trying times in the nineteenth century.

Familia always strives to include a balance between historical matters and material more specifically genealogical. In this respect it is particularly nice to be able to present three items written by serious genealogists on both sides of the Atlantic. Lee K. Ramsey's research outlines the use of records in the eighteenth and early nineteenth centuries from which other Ulster-Scots researchers can only benefit. James Bartlett's account of Friar's Bush, the oldest Catholic burying ground in Belfast, reminds us of the research interest in gravestones. Paul Richmond is a young researcher whose innovative tracing of his own family in late nineteenth and early twentieth century Belfast, at a time when the great majority of the city's 350,000 inhabitants had been born elsewhere, may come to be regarded as a model of its kind.

The reviews will bring our readership up to date with informed commentaries on a selection of the most recent publications in the fields of history and genealogy. As is the case with the principal contributors, there is a healthy breadth of interests represented, including professional and family historians on both sides of the Atlantic, just the way it should be in a publication whose audience reflects the migratory flow over the last three centuries that lies at the heart of our shared interest.

TREVOR PARKHILL
KEEPER OF HISTORY
ULSTER MUSEUM

FAMILIA

NOTES ON CONTRIBUTORS

JAMES BARTLETT is the Los Angeles correspondent for *Daily Ireland*, and has published in *Variety, History Ireland, Fortean Times, The Historian* and numerous LA publications

ANNE CASEMENT's research, since gaining a Ph.D. from Queen's University, Belfast, has focused on the management of Ulster landed estates, particularly the Londonderry family

W. H. CRAWFORD is a former Assistant Keeper in PRONI, a former Keeper of Material Culture, Ulster Folk & Transport Museum amd UHF Vice-Chairman

MARTIN DOWLING is currently an Institute of Ireland Research Fellow, Institute for the Study of Social Change, University College Dublin

EULL DUNLOP is a former teacher involved in researching and publishing local history in mid-Antrim and beyond

PETER GILMORE is a Ph.D. history researcher at Carnegie Mellon University, Pittsburgh, Pennsylvania, where he studying with David W. Miller

KENNETH W. KELLER is Professor of History at Mary Baldwin College, Staunton, VA

A.P.W. MALCOMSON is sometime Director and Deputy Keeper, Public Record Office of Northern Ireland

WILLIAM J. McGIMPSEY is a licensed engineering consultant and White family independent researcher who lives in Mahopac, NY

EAMON PHOENIX is Senior Lecturer in History, Stranmillis University College, Belfast

LEE K. RAMSEY, family historian and council member of the Scotch-Irish Society of USA, lives in Dallas, GA

J. FRED RANKIN, a retired businessman, has published extensively on ecclesiastical history and serves on the Publications Committee of the UHF

PAUL RICHMOND has just graduated from Queen's University, Belfast with First Class Honours in English and has published in *North Irish Roots* and local newspapers

A.T.Q. STEWART is a former Reader in Irish History at Queen's University, Belfast

TREVOR PARKHILL is Keeper of History, Ulster Museum, Belfast and Editor of *Familia*

'If they would come to America'
Inheritance as a form of chain migration

PETER GILMORE

The nearly 1,000,000 emigrants who left Ireland for the United States between the close of the American Revolution and the Great Famine had various reasons which ultimately led to their relocation.[1] In the case of at least a few, the promise of property bequeathed to them in the wills of relations who had emigrated to America previously added significantly to the case for boarding emigrant ships. This article will examine examples of this practice (evident in the wills made by settlers of Ulster origin) derived from wills made in western Pennsylvania in the first half of the nineteenth century.

Migration through inheritance may be thought of as a form of chain migration, in that those who had already migrated and had established themselves provided the means by which others could migrate. This is, generally speaking, what scholars of migration have identified as chain migration: patterns of movement in which those who have relocated assist family and friends to make the move through advice, encouragement and financial support. Chain migration was a major factor in Irish immigration to the United States. As Patrick Fitzgerald observed in the last issue of this publication, 'Wherever you travel in Ireland you are soon reminded of the pervasive influence of chain migration. There was little sporadic or random about the developing patterns of emigration from Ireland.'[2] That would appear to be no less true for Presbyterian emigrants from Ulster. The editor of *Familia* has pointed out elsewhere, the evidence from migrant letters from Ireland's northern counties suggests that a system of chain migration was operative by the 1830s, possibly derived from the improved communications in place pre-1775.[3]

Examples of Ulster immigrants established in America who bequeathed property to family back home in Ireland have been found for the colonial period. 'Virtually every Scots-Irish colonist had at least a few relatives who had remained in Ireland', according to Kevin L. Yeager. 'The occasional bequests of property by Pennsylvania Scots-Irishmen to family members in Ulster reflected this continued transoceanic bond of kinship'. Yeager's 2000 doctoral dissertation cites four wills made in Lancaster County in the 1740s.[4]

Throughout the eighteenth century, families of Irish origin moved westward across the southern tier of Pennsylvania, overcoming the natural boundaries of mountain ridge and river. From Lancaster, Chester and other eastern counties in the first half of the century, the primary focus of Ulster settlement became the Cumberland Valley (the present Cumberland and Franklin counties) in the 1760s. By the eve of the American Revolution, a precarious string of European settlements had been constructed west of the Allegheny Mountains. The ensuing hostilities slowed the flow of Irish settlers across the mountains just as it halted Irish emigration across the Atlantic. Most of our examples of wills come from Irish immigrants who located west of the mountains in the Pittsburgh area shortly before or not long after the American Revolution.

The well-travelled and apparently successful John Campbell, a native of County Tyrone, owned property in Virginia and Pennsylvania; his will was approved by a court in the State of Kentucky and recorded in Allegheny County, Pennsylvania in 1800. He bequeathed passage money to his sister Sarah Beard and her children if they and a half-brother, Allen Campbell, would come to America.[5] Similarly, James McClelland of Pine Township, Allegheny County, in his will of 1803 provided for passage money for his sister Mary Kirkpatrick and her children.[6]

Not all would have availed themselves of the opportunity, as the following case reminds us. James McFarlane, originally from Eskragh, parish of of Killeeshil, barony of Dungannon, County Tyrone, had served in the American military during the Revolution and acquired land and social status in Washington County in south-western Pennsylvania. He was a miller by trade, and relatively well-to-do. McFarlane's neighbours confirmed his leadership by electing him as a major in the Mingo Creek militia. This proved something of a death warrant: leading the militia in its attack on the mansion of a hated revenue official, McFarlane received a fatal wound. He thus became one of the few casualties of the Whiskey Insurrection of 1794.[7]

Among McFarlane's heirs was a brother, Hugh, still resident in County Tyrone. In 1798 Hugh and his wife sold their share of the deceased sibling's estate for £250 (in Pennsylvania currency) to another brother Andrew, already resident in Pennsylvania. If James McFarlane did not promote the chain-migration process posthumously, he did so while alive. In 1789 he signed an indenture paper pledging to teach Samuel Scott of Crilley, parish of Aghaloo in County Tyrone 'the farming business'. Young Scott was to dwell and serve with him for six years 'from the time of his arrival in the Neighbourhood of Pitts Burgh in Pencilveny'. The Washington County miller paid for the emigration of another Ulsterman; the estate records detail the cost of the purchase of stores in Londonderry and passage for a John Reed. It is not certain to whom the estate papers refer when recording the expense of 'Indenture & bond of a Servant lad who ran away immediately after the decease of his Master and was never since taken nor did they ever receive any thing for his time and passage ...[8]

Our next three examples are more detailed, and confirm that the intended beneficiaries of inheritance did in fact emigrate following the recording of the wills. Hugh Alexander arrived in Pennsylvania sometime prior to the start of the American Revolution in 1775; his name appears in Cumberland County records as a surveyor and schoolmaster in Shippensburg in 1776 and in Carlisle in 1779. Like many others, he moved westward across the Allegheny Mountains not long after the war's conclusion; there, beginning in 1788, he bought twenty-two tracts and purchased the largest of five tracts between the Monongahela and the Allegheny Rivers in what is now Pittsburgh and its eastern suburbs.[9] Alexander raised cattle, sheep, hogs and horses on his extensive farm holdings.[10] He associated with others who had moved westward from the largely Scots-Irish Cumberland Valley in south central Pennsylvania shortly after the war and seized the timely opportunity to obtain land.[11] He appears to have been linked to distinguished citizens also through Beulah Presbyterian Church, until 1828 the first Presbyterian congregation immediately to the east of Pittsburgh.[12]

That he gained some stature among his peers is indicated in the notice of his death, rare for the time, which appeared in the Pittsburgh *Gazette* on 17 September 1813:[13]

> DIED, on Friday the 3d inst. at his farm in Pitt township, at an advanced age, HUGH ALEXANDER, Esquire. The death of Mr. Alexander will long be remembered with great regret by his relatives and acquaintances, to whom he was endeared by his amiable disposition and many virtues. His feelings were ever ready to sympathize with the unfortunate, who never appealed in vain to his humanity. His prospects and hopes of futurity were of the most consoling nature. His life was blameless – his death triumphant.[14]

Hugh Alexander's will, written in 1792 and recorded by the Allegheny County Recorder of Wills on 10 January 1814, divided his property amongst his brother James, sister Agnes and stepfather John Blain, and required their support of his mother, Rosanah Blain. Apart from 200 acres in north-western Pennsylvania left to one Thomas Cousins ('if he serves out his Indenture'), following the deaths of these three principal beneficiaries the Alexander estate was to go to the sons of his first cousin, William Alexander of Ballylagan, Ballynure parish, barony of Lower Belfast, County Antrim.[15]

Most likely, Hugh Alexander's mother, stepfather and sister had predeceased him; certainly none of them are mentioned in the will of his brother James Alexander, recorded in November 1821. However, that document reveals that in the nearly thirty years since Hugh's will was written, one of the sons of cousin William Alexander had died without children. On that basis James asserted his right to half of his brother's estate, which he bequeathed to his friend James Horner. He named his 'trusty friends' Dunning McNair (the brother-in-law of James Horner), David Little and the fortunate Horner himself as executors.[16] Nonetheless, the cousin's son William Alexander, his wife and children arrived in Allegheny County to claim their second cousin's legacy.

Little information is readily available about William Alexander's life prior to emigration. The parish of Ballynure in 1821 had a population of 2,759.[17] The townland of Ballylagan was one of nine owned by Conway Dobbs, Esq. whose rents in the following decade appear to have been the highest in the parish. Linen *circa* 1820 was a mainstay of the local economy, affording, in its various branches, employment and excellent means of support to all the females and the major portion of the male population', and would continue to do so for another decade or so. Where some '600 persons' were employed in the linen trade in the village and neighbourhood of Ballynure in the early 1830s, 'not 50 hands' were reported employed in the neighbourhood in 1837.[18] Alexander, who became a linen merchant in Pittsburgh, was among those involved in the linen trade in Ballynure. As the Alexanders made their move, Ulster's economy experienced a steep decline in agricultural prices, complicated by the gathering collapse of the rural linen industry through consolidation and mechanisation.[19] Certainly under these conditions the prospect of unencumbered title to property in America would be a tempting offer, if not a lifeline for a weaver and his large family.

The Alexander family arrived in Pennsylvania in 1821 by way of Canada. Sailing on the brig *Superior* from St. Andrew's, New Brunswick to Philadelphia were William Alexander, age 44, weaver; his wife Elizabeth, age 38; and ten children, the eldest 18 years of age.[20] This may have been the William Alexander, described as a farmer from Belfast, who applied for naturalisation in the Allegheny County courts in 1823 and was naturalised on 9 October 1826.[21] The owner of the Alexander estate, 'Lemington', was recalled as a linen merchant and Presbyterian; the wholesale dry goods company in Pittsburgh in the 1830s associated with merchants named Alexander may well have been launched with the bequeath of immigrant farmer Hugh Alexander.[22] The *Directory of Pittsburgh and Allegheny Cities* for 1862 lists a William Alexander as a 'gentleman'; quite possibly the fifteen year-old emigrant of forty-one years earlier.[23] In time another son of weaver William – named Hugh, possibly for their benefactor – inherited at least a portion of the property once owned by his namesake.[24]

The second detailed example is the story of a County Monaghan man who likewise left a legacy to a cousin back home. John Nesbit was one of two first-cousins of that name who settled in south-western Pennsylvania. One, resident in the region by 1790, had achieved some recognition as a Presbyterian elder.[25] The other, with whom we are concerned, farmed in Moon Township in western Allegheny County (to the west of the City of Pittsburgh). The 1820 United States Census records his household as consisting of a male and a female, both over 45 years of age; a 'foreigner not naturalised' and a 'person engaged in agriculture', both of whom may have been this same John Nesbit.[26] Apparently a man of deep religious values, like his somewhat better known cousin, this John Nesbit took care of an ailing immigrant from County Fermanagh and thus was remembered in the will of David Mawger of Robinson Township.[27]

John Nesbit died in 1837. In his will, he left to his wife Margaret 'all the rents issues and profits of my plantation during her natural life for her support, and likewise my personal property and money'. In addition, Nesbit bequeathed to his cousin, 'Charles Hagan of Tullykenny, parish of Drumsnat and County of Monaghan in Ireland that part of my plantation' on which he was living 'in fee simple without any incumbrance [sic]' after his wife's death. Should Hagan (or Hagen) arrive while his widow still lived, Nesbit wrote, she would be as his tenant; her payment to him of $100 would enable Hagan 'to begin farming if he shall choose to live on the place agreeable to the above terms'. Should he not arrive until after the widow's death, he would not receive the $100, but would be in receipt of 'the profits of the place from her decease'.[28]

The southern half of Nesbit's estate contained his residence. The northern part, 'whereon John Hanlon now liveth', was to be sold after his wife's death 'to the best advantage'. Of the profits, $130 was to be divided between the Presbyterians' Theological Seminary and Western Missionary Home Society, with the remainder to be shared by the five sons of his cousin John Nesbit. The will was witnessed by John and Benjamin Hanlon; executors were David Nesbit, son of cousin John, and James Craig.[29]

Charles Hagen accepted the bargain, moving from one rural neighbourhood to another. The parish he left in 1841 had a population of 1,724 and 667 families, a marked decrease from the population of 2,518 recorded in 1821.[30] The general conditions that characterised east Ulster *circa* 1820 (as described above) would have applied to the west in 1840; the prospect of good farming land, unencumbered, may have seemed a good deal indeed.

The 1840 U.S. Census confirms that Charles Hagen resided in Moon Township, the household consisting of a male, aged 50 to 60, a female aged 30 to 40, and four boys, all under 15 years of age.[31] The Hagens benefited further from the will of Nesbit's widow. Margaret Nesbit, who died in 1840, bequeathed to her husband's cousin 'all the money in his hands for which I hold his notes. This legacy is given as a consideration for the kind attention paid me by C. Hagen and wife [Ann] during the time I have lived in their family'. Mrs Nesbit's nieces Jane Walker and Sarah Reed received various blankets, sheets, dresses and shawls. Otherwise, all of the widow's clothes went to Ann Hagen, as well as 'bed, bedding and household furniture and articles of every description'. All monies remaining after expenditure on funeral and doctor expenses were left to the trustees of the Western Theological Seminary. Charles Hagen received an additional legacy: 'Thirty Dollars to be paid by my executors', from debts collected by the executors.[32]

The Nesbits' heir was quite possibly the same Charles Hagen, a native of Ireland, who applied for naturalisation in 1844 in Allegheny County.[33] But it is not clear that he was in fact naturalised, nor is it at all clear how the Hagens fared in their new home. While there is no indication that the property was sold during the next several years, neither does Charles Hagen again appear in the next U.S. Census for Allegheny County. However, a Charles Hagen, 'gentleman', was living in Allegheny city (now the north side of Pittsburgh) in 1862 – possibly a successful conclusion to a story that began with a remembrance by a (physically) distant relation.[34]

The details associated with the third and final example are uncertain and inconclusive, and surprising in their unexpected direction, a circumstance which tends to limit its usefulness for this discussion but may also add to its interest. In an article heretofore largely dominated by men, the principals here are two women named Esther. Also of particular relevance to this example is a connection with the Associate

Reformed Church, a dissident Presbyterian denomination which attracted recent immigrants.

Information about the life of Esther Kerr Willock is unfortunately scanty. She was married to a man at least twenty years her senior.[35] Andrew Willock was apparently among those Ulstermen who arrived in the Pittsburgh area after the close of the Revolutionary War. He sponsored near-relations, Alexander and Noble Willock, when those Irish-born brothers applied for naturalisation in 1799. Alexander Willock arrived in Pittsburgh in 1792 and worked as a baker and innkeeper in the village until he saved up enough money to buy two hundred acres of land in Mifflin Township, Allegheny County; Andrew Willock had a boot and shoemaking shop in Pittsburgh.[36]

Andrew Willock's death in January 1836 received a brief mention in the *Pittsburgh Gazette*; the newspaper remarked that he was 'long a respected citizen of Pittsburgh, in the eighty-first year of his age'.[37] Willock's will mentions a son, John, and his wife Esther, with bequests to 'my girl, Mary Gorman, now living with me, when 18' and to Alexander, the son of his relation Alexander Willock of Mifflin Township.[38]

Esther Willock died nearly nine years later, in November 1844; she was then living just across the Allegheny River from Pittsburgh, in Allegheny city. Her will contained no reference to her son, who later sued her estate. She made bequests to the Rev. John Pressly, for the use of the Foreign Missionary Society of the Associate Reformed Church; to her brothers, John and Robert Kerr; to her sisters, Ann and Margaret, in Ireland, 'two miles from Dungannon'; and if neither were living, to her niece Esther, daughter of Samuel Kerr, near Dungannon; to Samuel Morrow, a tailor of Allegheny City; and to the sons and daughters of her brother Robert. Young Esther was also to receive 'Fifty dollars, to be kept at interest until she comes of age' and the widow's bed and bedding and six silver spoons.[39]

A brief reference to her brother John (and a clue to a possible date of emigration for Esther) may be contained in the correspondence of a County Antrim emigrant of the same name. John Kerr wrote his uncle in Ulster that 'There are a great many persons in Pittsburgh & the neighbourhood of the name of Kerr, many of whom came from

Ireland'. Among these, he said, was the man with whom he boarded, 'a namesake of my own of the name of Kerr, from the county Tyrone.' In a subsequent letter he said he resided in the house of a man named Kerr: 'he is from Dungannon, County Tyrone, Ireland, and came to this country in the year 1801.' Possibly by coincidence, John Kerr the correspondent identified and associated with clergy and members of the Associate Reformed Church, just as Esther Kerr Willock had done.[40]

Apart from an appraisal of the 'contents of Trunk bequeathed to Margaret Kerr & Ann Kerr, Ireland', the accounts of the estate executors are silent with respect to the widow's Irish bequests.[41] They were apparently not made. Esther Kerr, the widow's niece, travelled to Pennsylvania to gain her legacy upon reaching age twenty-one on 21 October 1859, and attempted to obtain her bequest from the surviving executors. Failing in these efforts, she appeared in Allegheny County Orphans Court in 1860 to obtain a court order. Executor James M. Walker admitted in an October 1860 affidavit the veracity of young Esther's claims, nonetheless sought a dismissal of her case with the claim that he was never directly involved with the other executors in managing the Willock estate. The court, however, granted 'a rule to show cause why an attachment should not issue against J. Walker Surviving Executor of Esther Willock'. The court ordered Walker and Davidson to appear in court to answer charges on 17 November 1860.[42]

Alas, the record gives no indication of the dispute's resolution. We can only be certain that Esther Kerr, a young woman unable to sign her own name, followed the transoceanic path of a namesake aunt in the hopes of bettering her circumstances in America.

As well as representing a form of chain migration, legacies may also be considered as a transatlantic dimension of traditional inheritance patterns. Although impartible inheritance eventually came to be the norm in Ireland in the nineteenth century, Ulster farmers typically divided their holdings amongst their sons prior to 1815. As W.H. Crawford has observed, 'the inheritance customs of both Scots and Irish provided for all the family' on their tenant holdings. Lacking children, Hugh Alexander proposed dividing his legacy amongst his brother and his cousin's children; rejecting her son, Esther Willock sought to divide her estate among brothers, sisters, niece and nephews. Significantly, Hugh Alexander, John Nesbit and Esther Willock all emigrated from Ulster at a time in which the strength of home linen production made small holdings and partible inheritance possible.[43]

For the genealogist, an obvious drawback of wills as a tool for exploring chain migration is that not every emigrant produced a legacy that could meet the hopes and expectations of posterity! Thomas Mellon, an Ulster emigrant who amassed a fortune and bequeathed wealth, power and status to his progeny, is singular precisely because his achievement was atypical. Numerous immigrants assumed responsible positions in business, finance, politics and the professions, but many more laboured long without obtaining wealth, fame or even the modest bequeaths a widow like Esther Willock could bestow. Perhaps more typical than the Mellon saga was the story of Thomas Johnston, who made a good living for his wife and family hauling baggage for canal boats until hard work and hard drinking led to an early demise. His widow somewhat desperately contemplated sending daughter Isabelle to a cotton mill and son Robert 'to a trade as soon as he is fit to go', while hoping that relatives in Ireland might send aid – rather the reverse of the stories we have considered here.[44]

A conclusion suggested by these early nineteenth century wills is the existence of networks of kin and neighbours, business associates and work-mates that bound immigrants and potential emigrants on each side of the Atlantic and across the ocean as well. The close proximity in Allegheny County of John Nesbit, the County Monaghan man, to Hanlons and Maguires may be no more coincidental than the contact he and his namesake-cousin obviously maintained with family back home. Transatlantic communication also connected Alexanders and Kerrs. It is fashionable in some circles to see 'rugged individualism' as a primary characteristic of America's Scots-Irish; however, upon closer examination of the record, it seems more likely that the Irish in general, like other European immigrants in the United States, relied more on the kindness and traditional communal relationships of family and friends to re-establish themselves and make a viable beginning in a new world.

NOTES

1   Kerby A. Miller has estimated the number of those who emigrated to the
    United States to be between 100,000 and 150,000 in the 1783 to 1814 period
    and between 800,000 and 1,000,000, 1815–1844. *Emigrants and Exiles, Ireland
    and the Irish Exodus to North America* (New York, 1985), pp. 169, 193.
2   Patrick Fitzgerald, 'Teaching Irish Migration Studies,' *Familia* No. 20 (2004),
    p. 83.
3   Trevor Parkhill, 'Pre-Famine Protestant, Post-Famine Catholic: Do Emigrants'
    Letters Reflect the Stereotypes?' in Collins, Ollerenshaw, Parkhill (eds) *Industry,
    Trade and People in Ireland, 1650–1950. Essays in honour of W.H. Crawford.*
    Belfast, 2005, pp. 159–60.
4   Kevin L. Yeager, 'The Power of Ethnicity: The Preservation of Scots-Irish
    Culture in the Eighteenth-Century American Backcountry' (Ph.D. dissertation,
    Louisiana State University, 2000), Vol. I, p. 80. Yeager cites the wills of John
    Barwick, 1742; William Gregg, 1744; Hugh McNeal, 1747; and James Murray,
    1747, found in Lancaster County Wills, 1729–1908, Record Group 4,
    Pennsylvania County Records.
5   Helen Hariss and Elizabeth J. Wall, compiler, *Will Abstracts of Allegheny County,
    Pennsylvania, Will Books I Through V* (Pittsburgh, 1986), p. 10.
6   Hariss, *Will Abstracts of Allegheny County,* p. 12.
7   Thomas P. Slaughter, *The Whiskey Rebellion, Frontier Epilogue to the American
    Revolution* (New York, 1986), p. 180.
8   Account of Andrew and Francis McFarland, Administrators of the Estate of
    James McFarland, in Administrative Account Books, Law Library Washington
    County, Pennsylvania. (The spelling of the surname as it appears in the record is
    inconsistent.)
9   Elizabeth M. Davison and Ellen B. McKee, ed., *Annals of Old Wilkinsburg and
    Vicinity* (Wilkinsburg, Pa.,), p. 76.
10 See note 14.
11 The executors of his estate were George Wallace, first presiding judge of the
    Allegheny County courts, William Steele, an Ulster-born merchant and
    Pittsburgh town official (and brother of a 1798 émigré, the Rev. Robert Steele),
    and James Horner, a neighbouring landowner. Horner came westward to the
    Pittsburgh area in 1786 in the company of his future brother-in-law, the politi-
    cally prominent Col. Dunning McNair.
12 The church is located in what is now Churchill borough, Allegheny County, so
    named because of the Presbyterian meeting house on the hill's brow.
13 Pittsburgh *Gazette*, 17 September 1813.
14 The Executors, Horner and Steele advertised in the Pittsburgh *Gazette* on 24
    September 1813 a 'Public Vendue' at the late Alexander's residence at which
    livestock, farm implements and household furniture would be sold. Pitt
    Township in 1814 embraced much of what is now the 'East End' of the City of
    Pittsburgh and its eastern suburbs.
15 Will of Hugh Alexander, Wills of Allegheny County, Will Book II, p. 25,

No. 24, Allegheny County Court House, Pittsburgh, Pennsylvania. In the will
the residence of his cousin was rendered as 'Bellylaggan near Bellyneur in the
County of Antrim.'

16 Will of James Alexander, Wills of Allegheny County, Will Book II, p. 262, No.
204, Allegheny County Court House. For Horner and McNair see Note 11.

17 Abstract of Answers and Returns, Census of Ireland, 1821.

18 Angélique Day and Patrick McWilliams, eds., 'Parish of Ballynure' in *Ordnance
Survey Memoirs of Ireland, Parishes of County Antrim XII, 1832–3, 1835–40,
Ballynure and District* (Belfast, 1995), pp. 68, 46, 64.

19 Samuel Clark and James S. Donnelly, eds., *Irish Peasants, Violence & Political
Unrest, 1780–1914* (Milwaukee, 1983), p. 148; Kerby A. Miller, *Emigrants and
Exiles, Ireland and the Irish Exodus to North America* (New York, 1985), p. 230.

20 Document No. 101155, Irish Emigration Database On-Line, Centre for
Migration Studies, Omagh.

21 *A list of immigrants who applied for naturalisation papers in the District Courts of
Allegheny County, Pennsylvania, Vol. I* (Pittsburgh, 1978), p. 5. Given that
William Alexander inherited a farm, that Belfast was not known for its agricultural production in the nineteenth century, and that Ballynure Parish is located
in the Barony of Lower Belfast, this could be our man.

22 The 1837 business directory for Pittsburgh and vicinity lists a W.G. Alexander,
wholesale dry goods merchant; the 1839 directory notes Alexander and
Stockton, in the same business.

23 *Directory of Pittsburgh and Allegheny Cities*, 1862 (Pittsburgh, 1852) p. 4.

24 *Annals of Old Wilkinsburg and Vicinity*, p. 78. This may be the same Hugh
Alexander who in the pages of the Presbyterian periodical, *Pittsburgh Christian
Herald*, for 12 February 1836 announced the formation of a partnership with
Thomas Pollock to make and sell 'saddlery and harness'. Three years later, the
partnership apparently dissolved, Hugh Alexander is listed in a city directory as
the burgess (mayor) of the borough of Lawrenceville (now in Pittsburgh, then a
suburb), where he continued in the saddlery business.

25 This John Nesbit was reportedly 90 years of age at the time of his death in
1845, which would place his year of birth in or near 1755. By all accounts he
was born in Ireland; his will asserted a claim to real estate in Drumoconner, Co.
Monaghan. He came to the United States some time before 1800. According to
one source, he was noted for his opposition to the Whiskey Rebellion of 1794
and elected to the committee that met with the United States Commissioners
sent west to resolve the dispute. (The same account describes him as among the
first elders of Montours Presbyterian church, established in 1778.)

26 United States Bureau of the Census, *Census of the United States, 1820*.

27 'Mawger' turns out to be a phonetic rendering of Maguire; the deceased father
(still resident in Ireland) was listed as Peter McGwire. Hariss, *Will Abstracts of
Allegheny County*, p. 18.

28 Will of John Nesbit, Wills of Allegheny County, Will Book IV, p. 395,
No. 254, Allegheny County Court House. The parish of Drumsnat is in the
barony of Monaghan.

29 Will of John Nesbit. 'John Hanlon and sons John, Benjamin, Hughey, James

and Joseph' were regarded among early (pre-1820) residents of Moon Township. *History of Allegheny County, Pennsylvania, Part II* (Chicago, 1889), p. A006.

30 *Report of the Commissioners Appointed to take the Census of Ireland for the Year 1841* (Dublin, 1842), p. 344; *Abstract of the Answers and Returns ...* (London, 1823), p. 304.

31 United States Bureau of the Census, *Census of the United States, 1840.*

32 Will of Margaret Nesbit, Wills of Allegheny County, Will Book V, p. 166, No. 132, Allegheny County Court House. She appointed as her executor the Rev. John K. Cunningham, minister to the Presbyterian congregation of Montour from 1830 to 1840. (*The Story of Old Montour, Montour Presbyterian Church, Steubenville Pike, Allegheny County, Pennsylvania* [by church?, 1925], p. 42.)

33 *A List of Immigrants Who Applied for Naturalisation Papers in the District Courts of Allegheny County*, Vol. 2, 1841–1855, p. 41.

34 *Directory of Pittsburgh and Allegheny Cities ...* (Pittsburgh, 1862), p. 117.

35 The age difference is indicated by the 1830 U.S. Census Report: one male over 60 and under 70, one female over 30 and under 40 years of age.

36 *A List of Immigrants*, p. 4; *History of Allegheny County*, p. A726; *Memoirs of Allegheny County*, Vol. I, p. 113; *The Pittsburgh Directory for 1815* (Pittsburgh, 1815; reprinted, 1905), p. 88. Perhaps coincidentally, Andrew's shop was located near to that of another shoemaking Willock, William, a native of Ireland who applied for naturalisation in 1808. (*The Pittsburgh Directory for 1815*, p. 89; *A List of Immigrants*, p. 93.)

37 *Pittsburgh Gazette*, 28 January 1836. The age is in conflict with the 1830 Census information.

38 Hariss, *Will Abstracts of Allegheny County*, p. 107. This information is consistent with that contained in the 1830 Census, which lists a male aged 20 to 50 and a female, aged 10 to 15, in addition to the married couple.

39 Will of Esther Willock, Wills of Allegheny County, Will Book V, p. 525, No. 425, Allegheny County Court House. The Associate Reformed Church, which represented a 1782 union of Seceders and Covenanters, proved attractive to many immigrants who had been affiliated with the regular Presbyterian Church in Ireland. The Rev. Pressly, a native of South Carolina, was pastor of the Associate Reformed Church of Allegheny (later, First United Presbyterian Church of Allegheny) for 38 years, beginning in 1833. All three of the executors of Esther Willock's will – Hezekiah Nixon, James M. Walker and William Davidson – were among the founders of the Allegheny (city) Associate Reformed congregation; Nixon and Walker were among the first elders. (*Seventy-fifth Anniversary of the First United Presbyterian Church of Allegheny, Pennsylvania, 1831–1906* [Allegheny, PA, 1906], pp. 12, 30.) Esther Willock's son John sued successfully to recover $130.71 from his mother's estate. ('Supplemental & final account of H. Nixon, Wm. Davidson, James Walker Executors of the Estate of Esther Willock decd. Dec. 27, 1847,' Orphans Court Records, No. 2 December 1847, Register of Wills, Allegheny County Courthouse.

40 Kerr Family Letters, 1843–52, MIC. 144/1, Public Record Office of Northern Ireland, Letters of John Kerr, dated 16 June 1843 and 23 January 1844, both

from Upper St. Clair (near Pittsburgh). (Typescript by Kerby A. Miller.) It is interesting to note that U.S. Census indices show a John Kerr in St. Clair Township in 1810 and 1830, and in Upper St. Clair (newly created) in 1840. John Kerr the letter-writer should not have been surprised; as Robert Bell observes in *The Book of Ulster Surnames*, 'Kerr is among the fifty most common names in Ulster and is found in every county.' (p. 113.)

41 'Account of Hezekiah Nixon, James M. Walker & Wm. Davidson Executors of the Estate of Esther Willock late of Allegheny City,' Orphans Court No. 7 March Term 1846, Register of Wills, Allegheny County Courthouse; 'Supplemental & final account'. The accounts included an appraisal of the silver spoons promised Esther Kerr.

42 Estate of Esther Willock, No. 54, Orphans Court, Register of Wills, Allegheny County Courthouse.

43 Miller, pp. 217, 202; W.H. Crawford, 'Ulster as a Mirror of the Two Societies,' in T.M. Devine and David Dickson, eds., *Ireland and Scotland, 1600–1850, Parallels and Contrasts in Economic and Social Development* (Edinburgh, c. 1983), p. 63.

44 Letter of Margaret Johnston to Robert Johnston, Irvinestown, Co. Fermanagh, 1846, Archives of Industrial Society, University of Pittsburgh, AIS 84:5; a photocopy obtained from records of the Northern Ireland Public Record Office.

The Management of the Londonderry Estates in Ulster during the Great Famine

ANNE CASEMENT

INTRODUCTION

IN THE AUTUMN of 1846, as the effects of the widespread attack of the fungus *Phytophthora infestans* on the potato crop in Ulster began to be felt, the Londonderry family of Mount Stewart, County Down, owned or were co-lessees of several significant properties in the province. These comprised the Ballylawn estate, near Manorcunningham on the eastern shore of Lough Swilly in County Donegal, an estate of almost 1,700 statute acres[1] founded upon land acquired by a Scottish ancestor following the Plantation of Ulster.[2] This was managed in conjunction with approximately 2,200 statute acres[3] west of Muff (now Eglinton) in County Londonderry, and some property in Londonderry city itself, acquired through a subsequent marriage into the Cowan family. In 1744 the Stewart family purchased the manors of Newtownards and Comber on the shores of Strangford Lough in County Down, which by 1848 had been significantly enlarged by the acquisition of adjoining townlands, together with the Florida estate near Killinchy, to comprise an estate of some 23,000 statute acres. In 1786 the family bought a half-share in a lease of the 23,000 statute-acre Salters' portion at Magherafelt in County Londonderry.[4] This was situated on the western shore of Lough Neagh, and was bounded, roughly speaking, by the settlements of

15

Castledawson to the north, Salterstown (Ballyronan) to the south and Moneymore to the west. In addition, there were two isolated townlands, Ballydermot and Edenreagh, in the parish of Ballyscullion to the north.[5] In 1834, Frances Anne (née Vane-Tempest), wife of the 3rd Marquess of Londonderry, acquired almost 9,300 statute acres[6] of the Antrim estate between Glenarm and Garron Point, and around Newtown-Crommelin, Dunloy and Clogh Mills in County Antrim from her mother, who was Countess of Antrim in her own right. Such widespread ownership throughout Ulster, coupled with the availability of agents' correspondence and other estate records, together with contemporary newspaper accounts, presents the possibility of discovering whether a uniform approach was adopted by the Londonderry family to deal with the famine and its effects on all its Ulster estates, or whether the individual circumstances pertaining to each estate governed the policy adopted, and, if so, to identify the nature of such circumstances.

In 1846 all the Londonderry estates in Ulster were the property of Charles Stewart, 3rd Marquess of Londonderry, who, during the Napoleonic Wars, had established a fine reputation as a bold and fearless leader of men. He subsequently enjoyed some success as a diplomat, culminating in his appointment as Ambassador to Austria, in which capacity he attended the Congress of Vienna. In 1823 he relinquished the ambassadorship,[7] and applied himself with vigour to the management of his own estates in Ulster and his wife's sizeable estates and colliery interests in County Durham. Although the couple spent the majority of their time in Britain, their interest and involvement in the management of their Irish estates are clearly evident from the agents' correspondence. Lord Londonderry's holdings were managed by agents under the overall supervision of John Andrews, who personally administered the County Down estates from the Londonderry estate office in Newtownards. His Derry and Donegal estates were managed by John Lanktree, who also had responsibility for Lady Londonderry's estate in County Antrim, and was based, from 1848, in the Londonderry estate office in Carnlough. The Salters' estate was managed by Andrew Spotswood on behalf of the 3rd Marquess and his co-lessee, Sir Robert Bateson, of Belvoir Park, County Down.[8]

Spotswood lived at Millbrook, near Magherafelt, formerly occupied by his predecessor George Bamber.[9]

John Andrews was the eldest son of a prosperous family of millers, linen bleachers and drapers from Comber, County Down. He commenced his working life in the family business, taking special responsibility for the orders and correspondence, but was also deeply involved in the management of the five-hundred-acre Andrews family farm at Carnasure on the outskirts of Comber. He and two of his brothers were passionate advocates of improved farming practices, and were active members of the Chemico-Agricultural Society, established in 1846. Since 1833, the family farm had been divided into a large and small farm, each being thorough-drained and managed on a rotational basis, including the cultivation of green crops for animal feed. The small farm, at seventeen acres, was much the same size as an average holding in County Down, and was intended to demonstrate how the principles of close-cropping could be applied on such a farm, utilising only simple techniques and implements.[10]

Andrews was appointed agent for the 3rd Marquess of Londonderry's estates in County Down in 1828. In 1833 his responsibility was extended to include the Derry and Donegal estates, and in 1834 to Lady Londonderry's Antrim estate also. This workload proved too much for him to manage to his satisfaction, and in 1845 John Lanktree took over the day-to-day administration of the Derry and Donegal estates, having assumed such duties for the Antrim estate in 1843. Nonetheless, Andrews continued to play a strategic role in the management of these estates, and his acquaintance with them gave him a thorough understanding of their tenantry, character and circumstances. John Lanktree had been previously employed as Andrews's assistant in Newtownards, and Andrews had sanctioned Lord Londonderry's decision to appoint him to the Antrim agency.[11] Little is known about Andrew Spotswood other than that he was responsible for several other properties in County Londonderry.[12]

Like the majority of men of influence of his time, Lord Londonderry believed implicitly that society should be organised on patriarchal principles: that it should be authoritarian, hierarchic, organic and pluralistic, and that every member of society had certain duties and obligations.[13] There were three principal sets of duties that the conscientious paternalist of superior rank felt he must perform: those of ruling, guiding and helping. A good paternalist was one who was both convinced that he knew what was good for his dependents and had the power to insist that his ideas be carried out. Furthermore, although the paternalist was conscious of the need for benevolence, the obligation to rule firmly and to guide and superintend was considered to be far more essential.[14] Lord Londonderry's belief in paternalism and of the obligations it placed on the landlord and tenant is clearly evident in his addresses to his tenantry and to the Newtownards and Comber Farming Society in 1841.[15] At the end of his address to the tenantry he begged, nay implored, 'the attention of his tenants to these his parental directions'. He was also a firm believer that if the tenantry helped themselves 'heaven will help them'.[16]

For his part, John Andrews thought it was the duty of those with sufficient means to support the impoverished:

> The line of separation between public and private charity is clearly defined. The state may, and perhaps should provide, that no person shall necessarily perish of want. The recipients of the bounty of Providence should think of their responsibility to minister comforts to those to whom the great benefactor has given a claim on their benevolence.[17]

He practiced what he preached – he and his family were amongst the leading subscribers to relief measures and other works of public benefit. Furthermore he felt that 'the closer responsibility and liability are brought home, there will be the greater circumspection'.[18]

There is a popular and widely held theory that upon his marriage in 1819 to Frances Anne Vane-Tempest, Charles Stewart became one of the wealthiest men in Britain,[19] and that this income was available to be spent on his Irish property. An annual income from his wife's estates of as much as £175,000 has been quoted by one local commentator,[20] but a figure of between £35,500 and £50,500 at about the time of his marriage is more accurate.[21]

Under the terms of the marriage settlement, Charles Stewart was obliged to provide for his wife's mother, aunt and children of the marriage; in addition great stress was laid on the need to apply his future wife's income to the improvement of her collieries. It has been estimated that the settlement only provided resources for him to bring the collieries into good working order, to look after family dependents and to spend £14,000 on his social life. Little or nothing was available to pay off the Vane-Tempest debts, to support his political patronage, or to acquire a London residence and renovate his wife's family home at Wynyard Park. Frances Anne's mineral wealth was precarious and required a great outlay of capital before it could be fully exploited. The only good security that could be offered for this purpose was the modest income from her farms in Durham (£10,500 in the 1820s), and after 1834 in Antrim (between £1,500 and £2,300 in the 1830s), and the already heavily mortgaged equipment of the collieries.[22]

Lord Londonderry's financial position in Durham thus forced him to rely substantially on his Irish income to meet his personal expenditure. From late 1834 onwards, he received a monthly allowance of £600 from the revenue of his Irish estates, and the stress laid on meeting these payments, promptly and in full, is quite evident from his correspondence with John Andrews. It is clear from the terms of the marriage settlement and the tremendous demands placed upon Durham income that English funds would not have been available for Irish purposes.[23]

All these factors – financial, moral and personal – influenced the approach adopted by Lord Londonderry and John Andrews to the famine crisis.

THE DOWN ESTATES

At the time of the famine, Lord Londonderry's estates in County Down enjoyed a national reputation for their quality and good management.[24] The property was in many respects one of the best situated and best circumstanced in Ireland, lying on the shores of Strangford Lough and comprising within its boundary two good market and post towns, Newtownards and Comber. Its inhabitants were 'an intelligent and industrious people, disposed and calculated to realise as large an amount of produce from the soil as its nature admits of'.[25] The majority of the land was under tillage, and there were only about fifteen hundred acres of bog, mountain pasture or waste land.[26] The 1837 Ordnance Survey Memoir described the farmers' houses in Comber as 'very respectable, whitewashed and slated', and the farmers in this parish as 'generally respectable men'.[27] Andrews in his submission to the Devon Commission of 1845 stated that the average size of farms in the district was twenty statute acres, and that agricultural practice had improved rapidly in the previous ten years:

> Farmers have begun within that time, many of them, to understand correctly the advantages of a proper rotation of crops. They have gone much more largely into the raising of green crops, and house-feeding cattle. They were always aware … of the great importance of draining.

Progress was slower with the small tenantry than in the larger men, as it was difficult to promote improvements amongst them. He regretted that although the condition of the labouring classes in Down, as elsewhere in the country, was not changing for the better, many of those farming thirty acres on Lord Londonderry's estates 'are living comparatively like gentlemen', as their houses and lifestyle testified; and that he had 'partaken of repasts at their tables as comfortable as I could have prepared at my own'.[28] His observation was echoed by the noted surveyor Maurice Collis who, except on Lord Londonderry's estates in 1848, had never in all his years of surveying Irish estates met a tenant ready without preparation to produce a bit of cheese, with bread, butter, and beer for an unexpected guest. 'This I met in almost every case where I was drawn into the homesteads of your lordship's tenants.'[29] Weaving was carried out to a great extent in Newtownards, with six hundred looms weaving cotton muslin, and one thousand women were employed embroidering muslin for Glasgow merchants.[30]

In his study of the effects of the Great Famine in County Down, James Grant concluded that the county remained remarkably free from its extreme effects, though that is not to deny that hardship was experienced by many of the population. To support his claim he noted the limited use made of the Government's principal form of relief in 1846–47 i.e. public works – Down being second to last in the table of county use of such schemes;[31] that local relief committees were almost the last to form; that the workhouses filled up less quickly than elsewhere; that, in common with most of east Ulster, the County Down Poor Law Unions successfully restricted their use of the Temporary Relief Act, and funded the aid they offered under its provisions with considerable independence; that the decline in population between 1841 and 1851 was 10.7 per cent, markedly below the national average of 24 per cent, and less than the Ulster average of 17.3 per cent.[32]

This conclusion is supported by John Andrews writing to Lord Londonderry in May 1847:

> Our soup kitchens are so far adequate to relieve the want which the workhouse cannot meet … The railway works … are taking the labourers whom the farmers, from want of money and dearth of food, have been throwing off, and the weaving in Newtownards is tolerably brisk, so that on the whole our situation is comparatively an enviable one, but our workhouse contains 750 in the body of the house, and nearly 100 in the fever hospital.[33]

The Antrim, Belfast, Newtownards and Larne Poor Law Unions were in fact the only four of the 130 unions not to participate in the Temporary Relief Act .[34] Many boards of guardians feared it as a great experiment in outdoor relief, with possibly nightmarish financial implications, but most were forced to adopt the measure because the cost of relief could not be met by local subscription.[35] Like the public works system, the soup kitchens had been designed to place the heaviest burden on local ratepayers, with supplementation of the rates through private subscriptions from local landlords and others. The Government's fiscal responsibility was limited to advancing loans to the finance committees (to be repaid out of the poor rates), and to making grants and donations, normally to be in an amount equal to the combined proceeds of rates and private subscriptions, though larger donations could be given in extremely urgent cases.[36]

Although the situation in County Down was certainly less critical than elsewhere, by January 1847 John Andrews felt impelled to inform Lord Londonderry that the distress of the poor was increasing daily. Considerable importations of food had been unable to satisfy the demand, or prevent price rises. Employment was not hard to come by, but families with no able-bodied member to work for them were suffering badly, and their number was great everywhere, including Newtownards. To alleviate matters, a good subscription had been raised in Newtownards and a soup kitchen would be in operation shortly. Although a great deal had been achieved by private charity in Comber, the same mode of relief was thought to be necessary there also. The raising of subscriptions had begun, coal had been purchased for sale at reduced prices, and a committee appointed to make arrangements for the soup kitchen, which was expected to be in operation in a few days.[37] Prior to this a ladies' committee in Comber had been responsible for relieving those in distress.[38] The demand for soup was great,[39] but Andrews felt that the nourishment it provided, together with a reduction in the price of Indian corn, kept destitution at bay.[40] On the Florida estate, the tenantry, backed by another local proprietor and clergyman, were about to aid the poor of that district. In urging Lord Londonderry to support their efforts, Andrews noted that although he had recommended the establishment of a soup kitchen, the area was a rural one and therefore the distribution of meal might be more practical.[41]

The effectiveness of these measures was graphically illustrated by articles in *The Banner of Ulster*. In the early weeks of 1847 a reporter from the newspaper was sent to areas around Belfast to assess the severity of the distress. Generally speaking, he painted a picture of extreme hardship and sickness. In nine out of ten visits he made in Newtownards he found the people had succumbed, or were succumbing, to dysentery. Measures to supply them with food, although satisfactory in a temporary sense, were not calculated to meet a crisis of long-duration. In four townlands nearby, which lay within or beside the Londonderry estate, he was informed that small farmers were limiting manual work on their farms to what could be achieved by their own families. The labouring population was suffering much as a result, and wages, if obtainable, were insufficient to meet the cost of adequate nourishment. He concluded:

> To say that the *whole* of the country over which I travelled is in a state
> so closely approaching to starvation as the cases I have described,

would be untrue. There are comfortable farmers in the district, but they are the exceptions, and the bone and sinew of agriculture – the labouring class – forms, unhappily, the rule.[42]

However, in the case of Comber (where the Andrews family were the major employers), he felt 'an amount of gratification which I have not yet experienced, except in two instances [Saintfield and Donacloney]':

> In the town and its immediate locality, extreme destitution forms the exception and not the rule, and instead of numbers being found idle while willing to work, the masses are employed and paid for their labour. It would be too much to assert that there is not much and pinching poverty in the town of Comber, but in nearly every case, if not, indeed, in all cases which I investigated, there were still some means, more or less, provided which 'kept the wolf from the door' of the indigent. After the many tales of distress I had heard, and the extreme misery of which I had been a witness for weeks past, it was a most agreeable relief to me to drop into the dwellings of a class of people who, although not being enabled to boast of a surplus of food, or perhaps even an ordinary sufficiency, were yet removed from pinching want, and generally in the enjoyment of health.

The means adopted here to relieve the poor were considered to be 'excellent'. They had been very successful, and the local inhabitants felt themselves placed 'in quite another position than before proceedings on their behalf were entered into'. The expenditure of the relief committee was about £8 per week, towards which Lord Londonderry contributed £10 per month. There was no danger of the efficiency of the committee's work being curtailed, due to a shortage of funds, as 'additional supplies can be raised immediately'.[43]

Andrews accepted that the Comber and Newtownards soup kitchens were 'much visited', and the poor and destitute were pressing on the workhouse 'beyond its powers of reception'. Thankfully, large arrivals of food had depressed prices for the present, but the 'future is veiled from the most penetrating human eye'.[44]

He was opposed to the Temporary Relief Act on several grounds:

> I hope we shall have nothing to do with it, unless the government shall contribute some gratuitous aid to the funds already under the management of our voluntarily constituted relief committees. To have

committees organized anew, under expensive surveillance, and to borrow money from government on the security of rates to be afterwards levied on tenants, and partially repaid by landlords, would incur wasteful expense, provable increased demands, under the presumed right to liberal aid from government funds; and, in the end, would tend to that demoralisation, which is engendered by a reliance on public aid; and would certainly extract from both owners and occupiers of rateable property a much larger sum than their voluntary subscriptions would require. On every ground, therefore, not omitting the credit of being able to get on without government aid, I would be glad that we should get on as we are doing.[45]

Statistics from the minute books of the Newtownards Board of Guardians show that by December 1846 the Newtownards workhouse had its full complement of six hundred inmates. By mid-February 1847 the number of inmates had risen to 832. Admissions in the following months were more than three hundred per month, with peaks in March and June. By February 1848 admissions had fallen to below two hundred per month, and continued at this level for the rest of the year. Thereafter, except for seasonal fluctuations, numbers fell back to pre-famine levels. On this evidence Grant concluded that famine-related hardship in the Newtownards union was sharp but relatively short-lived.[46] The Andrews correspondence offers support to this conclusion, as no mention of famine-related hardship is made after 1847.

The Temporary Relief Act was intended as an emergency provision only, aimed at bridging the gap between the winding up of public works and the passing of new poor law legislation in June 1847, to come into force on 1 October, in which there was provision for outdoor relief, administered by salaried relieving officers under specified conditions.[47] John Andrews's position as a local magistrate resulted in his being an *ex officio* member of the Board of Guardians of the Newtownards Poor Law Union. In 1847 he held views at variance with other members of the board, including most of the local landowners, over the legal provision of a right to outdoor relief. The board was in fact almost equally divided on the matter – seventeen guardians being against such a provision and sixteen in favour.[48] Andrews dreaded the creation of such a right as he felt it would 'immensely increase the number of claimants, and might in the end generate all the evils of the old English poor laws'.[49] Andrews thought that if outdoor relief were to be granted either in money, or in any articles of food convertible into money, whereby whiskey, tea and tobacco could be obtained, 'no caution or vigilance on the part of any board could prevent the most mischievous and demoralising abuses; and consequent increase of expense and charge upon the rate payers'.[50]

Though the famine years witnessed intense conflict between land-lords and tenants, they were both agreed on one point: the British government and Parliament had scandalously abdicated their responsibility for meeting a major share of famine relief after September 1847. Landlord hostility to the poor law system during the famine was thoroughly understandable. First of all they were responsi-ble for discharging the rates of every holding valued at £4 or less, and for paying half the poor rates of all holdings valued at over £4. Secondly, each poor law union was supposed to be self-financing, and landlords whose estates were located within the impoverished unions of the south and west felt deeply aggrieved that the burden of provid-ing for an extraordinary calamity like the famine should fall so dispro-portionately on their shoulders. They saw no reason why they should be held financially accountable for the peculiar geographical incidence of an event for which the responsibility should have been national and ultimately imperial.[51] Andrews obviously shared this view, feeling that:

> Nothing beyond temporary legislation should have been attempted ... the difficulties of the Government were great. 'Twere surely no easy matter to satisfy the people of England, when sums so enormous were to be demanded for Irish distress; but I fear Ireland will suffer for the expedients to which the minister has resorted to surmount his diffi-culties.

He also believed the new act would prove to be unworkable. In the south and west of Ireland it was already impossible to collect the exist-ing small poor rate – there could be no chance of collecting the high-er rates envisaged under the new law.[52] His fears were to prove justified, and reluctantly the government accepted that it was far beyond the ability of certain unions to finance their own poor relief.[53]

Andrews was anxious to delay granting outdoor relief until its effects on proprietors in other parts of Ireland could be ascertained, and felt that it would be impossible to prevent its commencement once relieving officers were appointed. His impassioned feelings against the implementation of outdoor relief rank amongst the strongest he voiced in his correspondence with Lord Londonderry. He felt it grossly unfair that measures intended to relieve the extreme conditions currently prevailing in the south and west of Ireland should be forced upon Ulster, and was prepared to do everything in his power to resist the Poor Law Commissioners, even allowing them, should they dare, to dissolve boards of guardians, such as that of Newtownards, who were able to support the poor under a proved system, but refused to saddle the union with the expense of unnecessary officers.[54] If overcrowding in the workhouse was unhappily a chief cause of mortality, 'Like the Downpatrick Board, we will build, and build, and in the mean time hire, and hire, but by some means we will protect ourselves against the "inundation" of outdoor relief.'[55]

The chairman, vice-chairman and deputy vice-chairman of the Newtownards Board of Guardians felt differently and tendered their resignations.[56]

> A law which treats poverty as a crime, and provides relief for the poor by forcing a man and his family into a workhouse, where confinement and restraint are nearly as great, and where the associates amongst whom he is thrown are almost as bad, as in our gaols and houses of correction, is I do not hesitate to say, both unjust and oppressive.[57]

In a summary of the controversy Andrews concluded: 'The commissioners may enforce the appointment of relieving officers, but they cannot prevent us from rendering their offices sinecures.'[58] Such appears indeed to be have been the case, for Newtownards was amongst the twenty-five unions not dispensing outdoor relief in the week ending 1 July 1848.[59] *The Belfast News-Letter* reported that many boards of guardians, especially in Antrim and Down, were determined to resist the appointment of relieving officers on the grounds that outdoor relief was unnecessary, and would be nothing better than 'an expensive practical farce'. The newspaper considered that the government was mistaken in thinking that outdoor relief was needed everywhere; and its enforcement was 'one of the most oppressive displays of arbitrary power – which could ever be contemplated in a free country'.[60] Perhaps, not surprisingly, the majority of the twenty-five unions not dispensing outdoor relief in the week ending 1 July 1848 lay in Ulster.[61]

At the time when the effects of the major failure of the potato crop in County Down in 1846 began to be felt, Lord Londonderry's financial position on both his English and Irish estates was extremely difficult. 1847 witnessed a severe economic recession in Britain, and interest rates rose alarmingly. This had an immediate impact on the management of the Irish estates. In November 1846 a major creditor demanded an increase of interest to five per cent. This demand was echoed by others to whom Lord Londonderry owed very substantial sums, and John Andrews predicted that an increase of interest to five per cent on all his Lordship's mortgages would add another £1,000 to the annual interest charge,[62] which in 1845 already swallowed £7,263[63] of the gross annual income of £22,694 from the Down estates.[64] A constant theme of Andrews's letters thereafter was the difficulty of meeting interest payments during the agricultural crisis of the famine and immediate post-famine years.[65]

The Down estates were liable to a variety of annual charges: interest charges on borrowings from a range of sources: Lord Castlereagh's[66] annual allowance of £3,000; salaries or rent charges for the agent, bailiffs, clergy and schoolmasters; office and estate expenses; crown and chief rents; and county rate and poor rate. These were met out of income from the rents, lead mines and turbary lettings, together with leet money. The cost of staffing, maintaining or cultivating, and improving (but not rebuilding) Mount Stewart house, garden and demesne was offset from the sale of garden and demesne produce and the letting of grazing land within the demesne. The surplus income (i.e. total income minus charges of all kinds) of both the Down and Derry and Donegal estates was routinely expected to meet any shortfall between the income and expenditure of Mount Stewart house, gardens and demesne; interest on bank accounts and agent's advances; and subscriptions. It also met election expenses. The remaining sum was

Lord Londonderry's own, and was used to provide him with a monthly allowance of £600 (i.e. £7,200 per annum), as well as meeting the living costs of himself and his household whilst in Ireland, and paying for special purchases for Mount Stewart.[67] The surplus income of the Derry and Donegal estates was insignificant compared with that of the Down estates, the former ranging during the time of Andrews's agency from nil to £894.[68] In 1846 the surplus income of the Down estates was £10,665. This fell by over £1,000 in 1847 to £9,338. The 1848 surplus was £9,792, and the figure for 1849 was £9,956.[69] The decline in the surplus of the Down estates in 1847 was due, as Andrews had predicted, to an increase in interest charges, coupled with a dramatic increase in the poor rate. The poor rate due for 1845 (payable in September 1846) was £447, the amount due for 1846 was £463, but that more than trebled in 1847 to £1,461. The amount due for 1848 was £866, and the 1849 figure was £638. By 1850 it had returned to a pre-famine level of £392.[70]

In early 1847 work began on the construction of the Belfast and County Down railway. Much of its route lay across land owned by Lord Londonderry. A loan of £12,000 to meet the cost of the substantial enlargement of Mount Stewart house, which had commenced in late 1845, was charged to the Down estates. Part of this loan was to be repaid with money raised from the sale of land to the railway company.[71] Under the difficult economic circumstances of the times, Andrews understandably wished to keep the additional charge on the Down estates to a minimum: he thus sought to obtain the best possible terms from the railway company. Negotiations commenced on 18 January 1847, and were not successfully concluded until May.[72] One local historian believes that substantial hardship could have been avoided if they had been concluded sooner.[73] It is known that admissions to the Newtownards workhouse peaked in March and June 1847,[74] but few able-bodied men are likely to have been within their number. Indeed, Andrews assured Lord Londonderry in February and March that there were very few unemployed able-bodied labourers.[75] However, a contemporary account suggests that the wages then obtainable by agricultural labourers were inadequate to sustain themselves and their families.[76]

In February 1847, Lord Londonderry wrote to John Andrews offering to stop building work on Mount Stewart if the agent thought it judicious,[77] but the income from the sale of land to the railway company, expected shortly, prompted a decision to continue.[78] The work cannot be seen primarily as a form of famine relief as it depended on the availability of skilled craftsmen;[79] nonetheless, in Lord Londonderry's eyes at least, it served to keep his people employed.[80]

Prior to the first attack of potato blight in 1845, Andrews had succeeded in bringing the arrears of rent on the Down estates 'into small bounds'.[81] At the financial settlement of September 1846, he reported that the arrear of rent of the previous November was £1,381,[82] but when the 1849 rents became due it had reached £4,296.[83] This dramatic rise in arrears was due initially to the potato failure which resulted in farmers replacing the potato in their diet with grain, which previously would have been sold and the proceeds used to pay the rent,[84] and in the loss of income from the sale of a pig, which, fattened on potatoes, formerly contributed to the rent.[85] This loss of income, coupled with rising interest rates, and the swingeing increase in the poor rate, were of extreme concern to Andrews 'Your Lordship will see how deeply these [charges] cut into the surplus, even if times were good; and rents secure; and how formidable the whole becomes when the very reverse is unhappily the case'.[86] Had the potato failure been a one-off occurrence, his concern would have been temporary, but in July 1852 he was forced to report the eighth successive manifestation of disease in the crop.[87] Such repeated blows, especially the serious attacks of blight in 1846, 1848, 1850 and 1851, reduced or wiped out the savings of the tenants,[88] and prevented the fattening of a pig. Nonetheless, despite Andrews's earnest exhortations against excessive potato culture, and encouragement to produce alternative sources of fodder for cattle and pigs,[89] it was not until 1850 that the cultivation of green crops had been significantly extended, and pork was beginning to be produced without potatoes.[90] This was fortunate, for other factors then came into play which further exacerbated the difficulties of farmers and their landlords. During 1849 the full repeal of the corn laws led to a decline in the price of every agricultural commodity. The tenant-right agitation of 1849–50 resulted in the loss of value of tenant right, which effectively prevented tenants from obtaining loans on the security of their tenant right, and made other creditors, such as shopkeepers, press tenants to repay their debts.[91] The effect of rising arrears on the solvency of the Down estates was offset, to some degree, by a substantial increase in the income of the lead mines.[92]

Early in the crisis, handsome rent reductions had been granted by Lord Downshire,[93] the leading landlord in County Down, and many other landlords had also reduced their rents. In a written submission for the Ordnance Survey in 1834, John Andrews stated that the rents charged by the Marquess of Londonderry in Comber parish were lower than those charged by any of the other landlords,[94] and Lord Londonderry did not concede reductions on the Down estates until late 1851.[95] He believed that his scale of rents had been fixed 'with a due regard to bad seasons as well as good', and that he had always adhered to the custom of tenant right. Furthermore, by largely forego-ing his income, a landlord 'may, possibly, sacrifice the convenience of others, which he is bound, in the first instance, to guard and superin-tend'.[96] Andrews felt any concession to the Down tenantry would have had a 'mischievous tendency',[97] by which he presumably meant it would have discouraged exertion and self-help on their part. This was also the view of Henry Wiggins, the experienced agent of the Grocers' Company, who noted that 'exertion is mostly very contrary to the char-acter and inclination of the tenant', and that 'abatement of rent is therefore what the Irish tenant is always seeking for'.[98]

It was customary for a tenantry to petition their landlord, respecting matters such as an abatement of rent, by means of a memorial, couched in suitably deferential language, in keeping with the paternalistic rela-tionship that Lord Londonderry, for one, believed should exist between landlord and tenant. In 1850, heady with the success of the tenant-right campaign, the Down tenantry chose instead to address their land-lord in more forthright terms. Their calls for a reduction in rent were refused outright.[99] When finally conceding a reduction in 1851, Lord Londonderry made it quite clear that his decision had been inspired by the increased willingness of the tenants to come forward with their rents, and not by any ability on their part to influence his actions by menace or abuse.[100] With hindsight, Andrews considered that it might have been more beneficial to have granted abatements and allowances at an earlier stage in the crisis. Fear of diminishing the income of the estate, heavily burdened as it was by the fixed payments described above, made him reluctant to do so.[101] He was only too aware that creditors insisted on prompt payment, and had a right to demand interest at an enhanced rate if payment was delayed.[102]

Clearly, Lord Londonderry and John Andrews cannot be accused of wearing their hearts on their sleeves, but neither can they be accused of complacency or indifference. Financial constraints made both men extremely reluctant to consider the rent reductions offered by other landlords. Nonetheless, Lord Londonderry suffered a substantial diminution in income resulting from the dramatic increase in the poor rate, his voluntary subscriptions to the Newtownards and Comber soup kitchens,[103] and, as the agricultural crisis deepened, mounting arrears of rent. Together with Lady Londonderry, he organised a number of charitable functions to provide funds for Irish relief, including a 'Grand Military Bazaar', which raised three hundred pounds.[104] He also provided extra employment at Mount Stewart,[105] and actively encouraged agricultural improvements. In 1824 he had founded and endowed the Newtownards and Comber Farming Society. Through a programme of instruction and competitions, and the provision of a library, it sought to encourage good practice amongst the tenantry.[106] In addition, in November 1846, he decided to aid the poorer and more backward tenants by offering a premium of five pence per perch for all drains executed on the Deanston system.[107] He made a further generous concession in February 1850 in the form of a grant of manure to the more backward tenantry, as an inducement to improve their farming practices. Andrews estimated the likely cost at over one thousand pounds.[108]

Andrews believed that the prime duty of an agent was to secure the future well-being of the estate and its tenantry, thus safeguarding the landlord's interest.[109] He was also a perfect example of an agent utterly convinced that the viability of an estate in the era of free trade depended on the successful adoption of improved methods of cultivation and husbandry. By his zealous advocacy of the gospel of improvement, and by personal example on his own lands, he left the tenantry in no doubt as to 'those farming plans and gainful ways, propounded by John Andrews'.[110] His personal experience of farming made him unusual amongst Irish agents, who, due to their elevated social position and education, frequently lacked a proper understanding of the problems of the agricultural tenantry.[111] Also his time in the linen trade had made him well aware of the need for a business to respond swiftly to changes in market forces. He adopted several strategies to encourage the tenantry to follow his advice. In 1847, he arranged with the Newtownards seedsman, Dickson, for the supply of turnip seed at the previous year's price,[112] and he invited deputations from the Derry and Donegal tenantry to come on an expenses paid visit to the Down estates to see for themselves the practices he was promoting.[113] He was also prepared to underwrite the sound adoption of green-feeding, believing that no loss could be sustained in so doing.[114] Furthermore, although improvements made by a tenant increased the value of his farm, and could thus make him liable to an increase in rent, this was not a concern of Lord Londonderry's tenants in Down.[115] Nonetheless, despite a lifetime's effort, in 1853 Andrews was forced to acknowledge that a man walking in any direction through most districts of County Down would find the table of improvements 'sadly disappointing'.[116] Such experience was commonplace. As one commentator ruefully remarked, 'intelligent management and good intentions were not enough. It was not merely that the Famine did come, it was also that farming remained … relatively backward and slow to change'.[117]

As well as giving advice, Andrews assisted the tenants financially. As he admitted to Lord Londonderry in May 1847, 'when we were not conceding the enormous abatements made by Lord Downshire and others, it has been impossible for me not to be accommodating in point of time'.[118] He was also in the habit of taking promissory bills from tenants whom he thought capable of redeeming them within a short period, and getting them discounted on his own credit,[119] 'I admit freely and at once, that my reliance on the value of tenant right led me to give aid to the tenants, and to exercise forbearance, and to involve myself seriously.'[120]

Andrews was quite clear that the most backward farmers would not survive the combined threats of free trade and the loss of the potato crop, and candidly admitted that 'my plan and object is to press those who are destitute of means to sell and emigrate'.[121] This seemingly callous and unfeeling statement was underpinned by the knowledge, firstly, of how much effort he had expended in encouraging tenants to improve their farms, and, secondly, by the fact that every tenant on Lord Londonderry's estates enjoyed the privilege of tenant right in its entirety.[122] With or without a lease, tenant right on the Londonderry estates in Down in 1845 was worth £10 per statute acre.[123] A tenant was thus in possession of the means of establishing himself elsewhere. When tenant right became worthless as a result of the tenant-right agitation of 1849–50, Andrews was the first to admit that:

> In such cases the resort to evictions, unless the sale of tenant right shall in some shape again become available, will produce an extent of suffering, and excite the public mind, and call forth a burst of censure, which it will be difficult to withstand.[124]

It is interesting to reflect that in public speeches made by two leading local tenant-right activists, neither took the opportunity to castigate Lord Londonderry or John Andrews for their treatment of the Down tenantry during the famine crisis. At an entertainment given by the Down tenantry to welcome Lord Castlereagh and his new bride in August 1847, Guy Stone, the vice-chairman of the Newtownards Poor Law Guardians who resigned over the course of action pursued by the board in late 1847, expressed sentiments akin to those of Lord Londonderry and John Andrews when he remarked:

> Because he [Lord Castlereagh] can appreciate our affection towards him better by our deeds than by our words; by our energy, industry, and independence during the late trying season; and I say it with all humility, by our charity to the poor, generously assisted as we were, by his Lordship and his noble parent; and by that just and honest pride that sustained us through all difficulties, and made us scorn to crawl to the feet of our English brethren, as supplicants, or to threaten them as sturdy beggars. By such deeds we show a regard for his Lordship and his interests, far beyond any sentiment we could convey in words.[125]

Likewise, John Miller, another tenant-right activist and member of the Newtownards Board of Guardians, took the opportunity at a dinner given by the Down tenantry for the 4th Marquess of Londonderry in November 1855 to criticise the 3rd Marquess for his stance in the rate-in-aid controversy, but offered no reprimand of his conduct during the famine crisis.[126]

In a report, compiled in the aftermath of the famine year of 1847, Maurice Collis acknowledged that in all his professional experience it had seldom been possible for him to offer those congratulations so justly due to Lord Londonderry for the prosperity and comfort of the tenants in every part of his Down estate, 'remarkable at all times, but more especially during the late season of almost unprecedented distress'. Out of a total of 4,050 rural and urban dwellings, only six had a value of under £3, only 158 of under £5 and only 403 of less than £8, and the remainder were of a much higher quality. There was remunerative work for all classes, 'the males at their trades or husbandry, the females at that description of lace making ... at which they are able to work in their own houses'. The cash yearly distributed through the tenantry from works executed in their own homes was over four times the poor law valuation, whilst the number of livestock was greater in proportion than anywhere else he was familiar with. Nearly fourteen hundred horses and approaching five thousand cattle were kept by the urban and rural tenantry, and the tiny number of asses and mules was another manifestation of their prosperity. Out of a total rural and urban population of 18,941, only 703 (3.7 per cent) of those over five years of age were uneducated,[127] compared with a national illiteracy figure in 1841 of 53 per cent of those aged over five years.[128]

In conclusion, Collis stated his belief that an examination of public returns, such as the 1841 census, would show that no other district in Ireland matched Lord Londonderry's estates in terms of prosperity, and no town had less poor quality housing than Newtownards.[129]

In 1851, the Dublin valuators, Byrne and Brassington, summarised the condition of the Down tenantry thus:

> The tenantry of this estate are industrious and intelligent, indeed it is very rare to find a property of such extent upon which the occupiers bear so invariably the stamp of comfort and respectability, and notwithstanding the potato disease having here made very serious advances, yet from the energy of the people, and their previous

solvency, its effects have been by no means so calamitous in this locality as in other districts where the crop itself has possibly not been so much affected.[130]

THE ANTRIM ESTATE

In his first report to Lord and Lady Londonderry, written in September 1844, when he had been merely a year in post, John Lanktree took the opportunity to describe the estate to his employers. About half comprised arable land, the remainder being mountain pasture or bog. The arable land was for the most part very inferior, as it was situated chiefly on mountainsides or places badly provided with roads. Much of the estate was largely unimproved, but if better farming practices were introduced the fertility and yield of the existing arable land could be increased, and additional land brought into cultivation, thus substantially increasing its rental value. In Drumcrow, where considerable improvement was already underway, he had given a ten per cent abatement of rent, in the form of a grant of lime, to encourage the tenants to continue their efforts. A new inland road was planned for Glencloy, where he had successfully reclaimed forty acres of waste land as an example of what might be achieved. The proceeds from reclaimed lands would be spent on planting and road improvements. In the parish of Ardclinis, survey work was underway to enable leases to be granted to individual tenants and rundale thus abolished. Lord Londonderry acquiesced to his suggestion to encourage the improvement of Carnlough by granting long leases for buildings. In Glenravel, he had gained possession of a substantial farm belonging to a tenant with long-standing arrears, who had absconded with all his stock and crop. Failing to find a suitable alternative tenant locally, Lanktree had brought in one from Newtownards, and supplied her with the resources to stock and crop the farm. He was delighted to say this farm was now a shining example of what could be achieved by the introduction of turnip cultivation in the area. Ballymacaldrick was the only locality giving him concern: here the tenants were heavily in arrear and complained that their rents were too high, which he suspected they were. A report was to be prepared, and the appropriate action taken.

Lord Londonderry had given him permission to use the modest funds raised from the letting of turf banks to provide an improvement fund for the benefit of the tenants and the estate, and this had already been used for the creation of roads and drains.

Most importantly of all, he had implemented a new system for the valuation of the land, upon which calculations of rent were based. As he so rightly noted, 'An error here either robs the landlord or ruins the tenant.' The new valuation was the consensus reached between himself and two of the most intelligent tenants, following a close inspection by them of each property. Several cases of extreme hardship had thus been relieved, whilst yet, he felt, promoting Lord Londonderry's interest. Respecting the collection of rent, as long as he could, he would advise, persuade or threaten, before he would have recourse to distraint or legal proceedings. He sincerely believed he was witnessing the beginning of better times for the estate: drainage work, turnip husbandry and dairy management had all commenced, and permanent improvements had been achieved.[131] His 1845 report confirmed this. About one third of the 258 farmers' houses were formerly 'promiscuously inhabited by the family and farming stock', and were filthy, smoky and badly thatched. Only two had a parlour distinct from the kitchen where the pigs were fed, and none had a comfortable bedroom. As a result of a grant of one hundred pounds offered by Lady Londonderry, twenty new houses and nineteen pigsties had been built, dramatically improving the quality of life of these families, and enabling pig manure to be conserved for use as fertilizer. The revenue from the turf bogs had been used to distribute thousands of thorn quicks and trees to create hedges for shelter; rams had been imported from Scotland to improve the sheep flock; and substantial progress had been made in the elimination of rundale. General distress had also been relieved by the distribution of clothing and blankets.[132] Lanktree was obviously a force for good, and the tenants were aware and appreciative of his efforts: 'Your Lordship's and Ladyship's wishes are carried into effect by an agent who has our real interest at heart, and under his active administration we have been stimulated to greater exertions.'[133] Although very willing to assist the tenants, Lanktree nonetheless expected them to repay him by striving, as best they could, to pay their rents and improve their farming practices. His training under John Andrews was reflected in his offer to underwrite any tenant who adopted a proper rotation and made cattle 'his chief study'.[134] Unfortunately for the estate, Lanktree's efforts came too late to offer much relief from the effects of potato blight, which, unlike in Down, first began to affect this locality significantly in late 1845.[135]

> No class felt the loss of the potato crop more keenly than the small farmers such as the bulk of the tenants on this estate, who cultivating small patches on the mountain sides depended wholly upon it for their living.[136]

Lord and Lady Londonderry paid their first visit to the estate in December 1846, and Lanktree described their reception thus: 'The respectful deputations from the several districts vying with each other in the loyalty of their addresses – the amateur band of the estate, the triumphal arches, the discharge of musketry, the blazing bonfires – all evidenced the delight of the warm-hearted people.' During this visit, the Londonderrys visited Ballymacaldrick, near Dunloy, where they were presented by the tenantry with a written address, which concluded with an appeal for Lord and Lady Londonderry's 'benevolent consideration' of the distress resulting from the loss of the potato crop 'the sole sustenance of ourselves, our wives and our children'. In his reply the Marquess, having recognised the loyal and dutiful behaviour of the tenants, made clear his belief that deliverance would come not only from renewed efforts by the tenantry to help themselves, but also from the desire on his and Lady Londonderry's parts to make proper arrangements to relieve them.[137] The latter were manifold: the remission of rent on all land under potato cultivation; the distribution of seed corn to the poorer tenants who had consumed all their grain in lieu of potatoes, and thus had none to plant;[138] the free distribution of turnip, carrot and parsnip seed;[139] the supply of large amounts of guano for the cultivation of green crops;[140] the establishment of a relief committee for Glencloy[141] which attended to every case of imminent distress, provided labour works for men and employment for women, and kept the price of provisions at pre-famine levels; and the promotion of drainage schemes to provide employment. In addition, Lord Londonderry provided funds to construct a lime kiln in Carnlough.

Not only did this dramatically reduce the cost of lime, which had been previously supplied at an exorbitant price from a kiln on a neighbouring estate, but it also provided jobs, a 'monument of his Lordship's paternal regard to the wants of his tenantry'. An agriculturist had also been employed to instruct and encourage the tenants.[142] Such aid was essential to farmers who in the harsh winter of 1847 were quietly consuming all their crops for the sustenance of their families and had no thought of rent, and for a community where oxen, sheep, fowl and turnips were stolen nightly.[143] Furthermore, the aid given for the planting of turnips markedly reduced the level of starvation on the estate in the following winter.[144] Not surprisingly, it had been possible for Lanktree to collect only three-quarters of the rent due that year.[145] In fact, prior to the May collection of rents, Lanktree warned Lady Londonderry that she must expect no recompense for her generosity, and meet the fixed charges and other disbursements (i.e. salaries or rent charges for the agent, bailiffs, clergy and schoolmasters; office and estate expenses; county rate and poor rate; together with subscriptions, the abatement of rent on potato ground and other allowances to the tenants, which in 1847 amounted to nearly £600),[146] until harvesttime. For him to obtain any significant payments of rent before then would result in the tenants being forced to sell their cattle, which would leave the grasslands ungrazed.[147] Lanktree, like his former boss, Andrews, was well aware that to force the sale of livestock would be 'killing the goose that laid the golden eggs … It is by stock of cattle, and that alone, that an estate can be improved, and fertilized, and a tenantry enriched'.[148] This was highlighted by Lanktree in September 1847 when he wrote to Lady Londonderry 'Butter which used to be the great resource of the tenants [for payment of rent] at this time, has hitherto been absorbed over the whole estate in small sales to purchase food'.[149]

Lanktree, again mirroring Andrews, strove to ensure that his poor law union was not placed under the jurisdiction of the Temporary Relief Act and new poor law legislation, thus avoiding a heavy rate being struck throughout the estate. Like Andrews,[150] he was conscious of the expense involved in the employment of relieving officers and other staff, the cost of which would support one out of every six paupers in the Larne union.[151] The level of distress within this union appears from workhouse statistics to have been less acute than elsewhere: although the workhouse could accommodate 780, the number of inmates recorded for either December 1846, December 1847 or December 1848 did not exceed 627.[152] Lady Londonderry was a keen supporter of soup kitchens, but Lanktree felt they could be of little use to such a dispersed tenantry as hers.[153] In the years 1844–6, three attempts were made by the Marchioness to establish soup kitchens, but 'the poor people did not come for it as numerously as could have been supplied'.[154] Despite Lady Londonderry's efforts at relief by other means, in 1847 Lanktree was forced to report three deaths on the estate from starvation.[155] Lanktree's efforts to avoid outdoor relief seem to have been successful, for the Larne union, like that of Newtownards, was among the twenty-five unions not dispensing outdoor relief in the week ending 1 July 1848.[156]

1848 was another difficult year for the estate. In May, Lanktree reported that a thousand acres of mountain pasture had been thrown on his hands, and there had not been a single response to his advertisement for graziers; no rent was expected to be paid until at least June;[157] the construction of Lady Londonderry's new residence on the estate was over-budget; and the poor rate was higher than the previous year due to the potato failure.[158] Moreover, the potato crop was expected to fail once more.[159] The year before Lanktree had predicted the ruin of the small farmers who comprised three-quarters of the tenantry, as too small an acreage of potatoes had been planted to support them,[160] and in his 1848 report he described how many of them had emigrated to America. Tragically, few succeeded in establishing themselves there: some were wrecked in the *Exmouth,* which had sailed out of Derry for Quebec, others succumbed to fever on arrival, or were robbed of the means of re-establishing themselves and forced to return home. The absence of detailed agent's accounts hinders the discovery of whether the estate paid the passages of the emigrants and/or bought up their tenant right. Nor has it been possible to estimate how many left the estate: the population of the area was not recorded in the 1841 census, and a calculation of the decline in the number of tenants would be misleading due to the prevalence of rundale on the estate.

Despite the efforts of some who remained to undertake draining and reclamation, stimulated and rewarded by free grants of lime, Lanktree had clearly become disillusioned by the failure of the majority to learn from the famine of 1847 and reduce their dependence on the potato, and grow more turnips.

> Their whole struggle was for the potato – turnips were quite a secondary object – many of them now see their mistake when it is too late – as their crop this year has been blighted also – which is the fourth year in succession.

The few who had heeded his advice and 'looked more to the produce of their cattle' had 'passed harmless out of the famine'.[161]

It is therefore surprising to learn that in January 1849 Lanktree met with a favourable response to his attempt to form a Farming Society, where the business of farming instruction would be made pleasanter by the provision of modest refreshments. Lanktree proposed a subscription of one shilling to meet the cost of refreshments, but a tenant's amendment was passed raising the subscription to two shillings, providing each subscriber could 'bring a lady'. As Lanktree noted, 'we are to have a regular farming ball', where he expected an attendance of more than two hundred.[162] Rents nonetheless continued to be difficult to collect. The estate rentals reveal that during the period 1845–8, when the annual rental was £2,800+, total arrears rose from £313 to £1,279.[163] In 1849, when a rebate of rent[164] reduced the rental to £2,544, total arrears rose to £1,963.[165] It is not perhaps surprising that Lady Londonderry, and more particularly Lord Londonderry, became dissatisfied with Lanktree's performance,[166] particularly in view of her Ladyship's past generosity and grant of a rent rebate. It is of interest to compare Lanktree's letters with those of John Andrews at this time. Although Andrews experienced a dramatic rise in arrears during the same period, and was also subject to the wrath of Lord Londonderry, he appears to have had a far clearer and fuller appreciation of the reasons underlying the difficulties experienced by farmers in realising their rent.

The other Londonderry agents, Andrews and Spotswood, were paid an annual salary,[167] but Lanktree was paid by the widely discredited method of a commission (five per cent) on rents collected.[168] His remuneration therefore depended on his exertions, and might have encouraged him to enforce payment. His failure to do so, combined with high personal expenditure,[169] could be construed as the motives behind his embezzlement of almost one thousand pounds from the Antrim and Derry and Donegal estates.[170] Part of this appears to have been money he pocketed out of rental received from the tenants, which he concealed by crediting to the tenants sums less than their receipts revealed they had actually paid.[171] This effectively made their arrear appear greater than it in fact was, and increased the likelihood of Lady Londonderry resorting to legal measures to enforce payment. Such behaviour, which resulted in his subsequent dismissal, sits ill with Lanktree's apparent sympathy for the plight of the tenants.

Discussion of relief measures was soon to relinquish centre-stage in Lanktree's letters to another topic, namely house-building. Lady Londonderry had a long-standing ambition to establish a residence on her Antrim estate. The restoration of Dunluce Castle was for some time contemplated, but this plan necessitated the establishment of sole title to the property, which could not be achieved.[172] A cliff-top site overlooking the Irish Channel at Garron Point, north of Glenarm, was chosen instead, comprising some of the finest land on her estate.[173] Lady Londonderry laid the foundation stone herself in February 1848, and the official housewarming took place in the summer of 1850, in the presence of the Lord Lieutenant of Ireland, Lord Clarendon.[174] The initial estimate for the building work was two thousand pounds,[175] but this was significantly exceeded. It has been generally assumed that the expenditure was met by Lady Londonderry personally out of the income of her Durham estates, but this proves not to have been the case. In the light of Londonderry policy respecting building costs at Mount Stewart, it is perhaps not surprising to learn that a significant proportion of the cost was met from the rents of Lady Londonderry's Antrim estate. This is borne out by John Andrews's statement that between November 1849 and November 1850 a large amount of Lanktree's and Cowan's [176] receipts were applied to the purpose of Garron Tower.[177] The burden was mitigated to some degree by the fact that some tenants obtained rent relief by assisting in the construction of Garron Tower.[178] What is perhaps more surprising is that Andrews's comment reveals that funds were also directed to the project from Lord Londonderry's estates in Derry and Donegal.[179] That such was certainly the case is shown by a summary account prepared by John Lanktree in March 1850, which reveals that the £957 spent on building work from November 1848 to February 1850 was met partly by three cheques from Lord Londonderry to the value of £160 and two bills to the value of £300, but most significantly by £500 from the Derry and Donegal agency account.[180] Unfortunately no detailed agents' accounts for the Antrim and Derry and Donegal estates have been found in the Antrim or Londonderry Papers in PRONI to throw light on how this was achieved at a time of extreme economic difficulty. Presumably it was charged against Lord and Lady Londonderry to be met out of the surplus income of the estates.

Garron Tower was built in Dunmaul townland, on land leased to the brothers Alexander and Stewart McAllister. Magill states that there were seven houses and fifty inhabitants in Dunmaul which 'were to be cleared to make way for Garron Tower',[181] and Dallat in his foreword to the same volume notes that 'the agent made light of the distress of the poor farmers who had been displaced in order that the project could go ahead'.[182] There is, however, evidence to suggest their concern may be somewhat misplaced. Lanktree states quite categorically that 'neither party [the McAllister brothers] would make any obstacle to the work on receiving a valuation for the land taken'. Indeed, Alexander McAllister had reason to be grateful to Lady Londonderry for she had found a place for his son at Seaham Harbour.[183] Both farmers would have received a capital sum to invest in the purchase of land elsewhere, at a time when land prices were plummeting due to the effects of the famine. Lanktree also describes the paid domestic positions at Garron Tower on offer to female members of the local community,[184] and it is not unreasonable to suppose that many other local people would have found regular paid employment in the gardens and grounds. Indeed, Magill notes that the houses at Dunmaul continued to be used for labourers at the Tower.[185] Employment would also have been available in the lime works established by Lord Londonderry, and for many the prospect of a secure regular wage was far preferable to the hand-to-mouth existence they formerly eked out as farm labourers. There would also have been many commercial opportunities for local farmers, fishermen and businesses to provide goods and services for the Garron Tower household. Indeed, at the laying of the foundation stone of the house, Lord Londonderry commented on Lady Londonderry's desire to 'spend amongst them ... part of the income she derived from their industrious labour'.[186] One Ordnance Survey Memoir writer remarked on the benefit to a community of the residence of the local gentry:

> It would cause the circulation of the very money the inhabitants of the village work so hard to obtain, would give a more healthy employment to many persons than their present one ... and induce some of the more wealthy persons to speculate by opening small shops and better inns.[187]

Lanktree wrote no annual reports after 1848, and was dismissed in 1850.[188] Regular reports by his successor Richard Wilson did not commence until 1858, thus making it difficult to form a detailed picture of the estate as it emerged from the famine crisis. Comments by Wilson in 1856 indicate that progress was being made, but it had been hindered by the small size of the farms which had to support large families, the high levels of arrears, and reluctance of the farmers to change their methods.[189]

THE SALTERS' ESTATE

Although this estate was located in County Londonderry, references by John Andrews and others to Lord Londonderry's Derry and Donegal estates appear to refer exclusively to the freehold estates, the estate leased from the Salters' Company being referred to individually as the Magherafelt estate. Such a distinction is logical in tenurial terms, and corroborated by the estate accounts where the modest Derry and Donegal rentals of about £2,400[190] cannot include the Magherafelt rental, stated to be £12,670 in 1845.[191]

An 1836 report indicated that the estate had always been well-managed, 'the lessees are good landlords, their tenants a very respectable yeomanry, and their lands are well cultivated'.[192] An 1845 report described the soils as being nearly all arable and of good quality, lime being available from two kilns on the estate,[193] whilst another in 1841 considered that the estate was let at moderate rents and the tenants were well-off. It also noted that the farmers were beginning to learn the value of occasional green crops, and iron ploughs, as well as other improved implements of agriculture, were coming into general use.[194] In March 1847, a Scottish agriculturist was appointed to assist their efforts.[195] The Ordnance Survey Memoir of 1836 described Magherafelt as 'thriving and improving', due to the prosperity of the linen trade and the increase of its markets and fairs. A flax-spinning mill had been established locally, and over one thousand weavers were employed weaving mill-spun yarn. There was a buoyant market for flax, oats, wheat, cattle and pigs. Considerable numbers of pigs were driven to Belfast for sale, some flax was exported to Dundee, and a good deal of oats was transported by lighter from Ballyronan to Belfast and Newry. Labourers were always in constant employment, and obtained high wages. Castledawson was less prosperous than Magherafelt, but nonetheless there was a thriving market for grain, butter and pork; a cotton manufactory gave employment to about eight hundred people in the surrounding parishes;[196] and labourers and mechanics were seldom unemployed. About 1822, a branch of the North-West Farming Society had been established to serve this area, and was perceived to have been of considerable benefit. The Memoir concluded that the inhabitants of the parish of Magherafelt were 'equal to any and superior to those of most of the neighbouring parishes, either in comfort, civilisation or morality'.[197] Parkhill has noted the dissatisfaction expressed by members of the clergy concerning the dearth of resident landlords in the area, who might provide leadership in a time of crisis.[198] The Salters' estate was thus somewhat exceptional in that Spotswood was a resident agent and a J.P., and thus capable of acting as an effective substitute for Lord Londonderry.[199]

Like Down, the effects of the potato blight did not become serious on the Salters' estate until the winter of 1846–7.[200] In early January 1847 none of the five workhouses serving County Londonderry was officially full. Although the Magherafelt workhouse reported 'no great pressure', nonetheless the number of inmates had increased by 250 in

December 1846.[201] By February 1847 the situation had become critical, and John Andrews alerted Lord Londonderry to the fact that the estate was one on which 'the small tenants are said to be starving, and where, at any sacrifice, employment in order to procure food must be given'.[202] A small number of letters exist for this period written by Spotswood to Lord Londonderry.[203] In March, he reported that the Magherafelt poor house was already accommodating more people than it had been designed for,[204] and that an outbreak of fever was raging in the work house and fever hospital.[205] The workhouse was then closed to new admissions, and outdoor relief was administered by Spotswood to about a hundred persons daily. Although the master and principal nurse of the workhouse had succumbed to the fever, Spotswood described it as being 'of rather a mild character', and was hopeful that, with the aid of extra experienced medical staff, it would be brought under control shortly.[206] Fever was still rife in the workhouse in May, and was on the increase in the countryside.[207] The situation was no better in October.[208] There is no Spotswood correspondence post 1847, but workhouse admissions revealed that the pressure on accommodation continued throughout 1848 and well into 1849.[209] There are, however, grounds for believing that many inmates may have been wandering poor.[210]

The severity of the crisis was vividly depicted in the letters written by another of Spotswood's employers, the Rt Hon. George Dawson, owner of the Castledawson estate, to Sir William Freemantle, one of the administrative staff at Dublin Castle. In January 1847 Dawson described the 'heartrending scenes of misery' on his estate, which with every expenditure within his means he could no more than most inadequately and feebly relieve. 'We are comparatively well-off in this neighbourhood; there is no want of food, but it is at such a price, as to make it totally impossible for a poor man to support his family with the wages he receives.' He himself had turned his kitchen into a bakery and soup shop to feed the mothers and children that clamoured at his door, and the gentry, shopkeepers and clergy were making every effort to help by incessant attention and subscription-raising, but 'what can be done when *thousands* are daily applying for one meal a day'. The area was overrun with wandering poor from the mountains or districts lacking resident gentry, and death was becoming commonplace. Nonetheless, there was still some employment available for weavers, and if the price of foodstuffs was to be reduced, mass-starvation could be avoided.[211] He was particularly struck by the patience and resignation of the people, who offered no violence or complaint, but felt that it was the will of God and they must submit to it.[212]

On the Salters' estate, despite the difficult times, the tenants were anxious to crop their lands. Spotswood, like Andrews and Lanktree, had procured supplies of turnip, parsnip and carrot seed, intending to offer them to the tenants at a reduced price rather than for free, not least because 'the charge against your Lordship and Sir Robert Bateson will consequently be much less'. Many of the tenants had requested a grant of seed oats, but as there were so many small holders on the estate he felt it too expensive to contemplate, except in some extreme cases. Sir Robert Bateson personally advocated a grant of flax seed, which was acceded to.[213]

Spotswood was not the only one to adopt such a pragmatic stance. In February 1847 he travelled to London to meet the Salters' Company, who expressed surprise at his reports of the extent of the destitution on the estate, as they were under the opinion that the north of Ireland had not suffered much from the failure of the potato crop. Nonetheless, they were willing to join with Londonderry and Bateson in promoting permanent improvements for the benefit of the estate, though a decision as to what form these should take would be deferred until the bills currently before parliament entered the statute book, or a definite proposal was submitted.[214]

Spotswood's position was undoubtedly an uncomfortable and difficult one. His letters reveal an obvious concern for the plight of the tenantry, but his ability to aid them was constrained by the high level of fixed payments for which the estate was bound. Lord Londonderry's half share of the rental (some £6,330) was expected to meet an annual rent of £250 to the Salters' Company; other fixed charges such as salaries or rent charges for the agent, bailiff, clergy and schoolmasters; office and estate expenses; county rate and poor rate; allowances to the tenants and subscriptions,[215] as well as annual payments to the Londonderry trustees of £3,230. Apart from jointure payments and the eradication of debts charged to the Derry and Donegal estates, these payments were intended to provide an accumulation fund to meet the cost of a renewal of the lease of the estate from the Salters' Company, or the purchase of other freehold estates in lieu.[216] The trustees had powers to demand payment of this sum, which they proved quite capable of exercising.[217]

In mitigation, Spotswood's letters reveal that, although rents were very poorly paid and arrears owed to Bateson and Londonderry rose from £9,824 in November 1846 to £18,048 in November 1849,[218] Lord Londonderry paid the poor rate and subscriptions to the soup kitchens in Moneymore and Magherafelt, and the Magherafelt dispensary. Additionally, he met the balance of the cost of seed sold to the tenants at reduced prices. Spotswood also appears to have offered an abatement to all those tenants who found the means to pay their rent.[219]

As in Down, the crisis on the Salters' estate seems to have been of short duration. In November 1847 Dawson noted that the area had been blessed with a superabundant harvest of everything except potatoes, and the latter deficiency was only due to the limited amounts that had been planted. All kinds of grain could be purchased at prices lower than previous years, and, so long as the employment currently available continued throughout the winter months, the people would have the means to purchase the cheap food. The transformation he witnessed in the prospects of the country as a whole quite confounded him, 'In the whole course of my life in Ireland, I never saw the farm sack yards in Ireland so full as they are at present'. He felt that the outlook for weavers locally was excellent. Although the English manufacturers were laying-off workers in Lancashire and Carlisle, they were sending over yarn to be woven in the Castledawson area in greater quantities than ever, due to the excellent workmanship and lower wage bills encountered there. Such was the demand, these manufacturers were forced to compete against each other for labour, and the price given for weaving a web of linen had doubled as a result. 'I came over here with fear and trembling lest I should be exposed to the dreadful scenes of poverty and starvation which I witnessed last year and to the constant appeals for charity – you will hardly believe me when I tell you, that with the exception of two or three professional beggars, I have not had a call for charity at my door.'

He considered that the poor law was being tolerably well administered locally, and with experience the guardians would make it effective and cheap. All the gentlemen and farmers he had spoken with were well aware of their duty to pay their portion, but were giving assistance where required, and discouraging the idle and profligate, in order to keep the rates as low as possible. The rates for the present year would be heavy, to meet the demands of the previous one, but thereafter should become moderate. Like John Andrews, he believed that this could be achieved by continuing to make the workhouse the test of relief, 'for it is impossible to conceive anything more strong than the disinclination of the poorest person to enter the workhouse'. He was thus sanguine about the prospects for his own area, but 'alas it is very different in other parts of Ireland, and I see no hope for them'.[220]

The 1848 harvest promised to be a bumper one also, but blight struck again in August.[221] Record yields of crops of all kinds were also anticipated in 1849,[222] and, by the time of a tour of Ireland undertaken by Dawson in 1850, pigs were again in evidence. So, too, were the signs of massive depopulation – no cabins by the roadside, the debris of former cabins, and quays filled with emigrants in Waterford.[223] In his own district money was more abundant, rents better paid and employment general. It was difficult to let land, and harder to keep a good tenant than to eject him. The markets were amply provided with pigs, extinct during the previous three years. There had been a partial potato failure, but people were beginning to see the mischief of relying on a crop which they had clung to with 'a desperate tenacity'.[224]

THE DERRY AND DONEGAL ESTATES

These estates appear to have been the most neglected of the Londonderrys' Irish properties. John Andrews attributed this initially to the fact that in his old age Robert Stewart, 1st Marquess of Londonderry, was unable to inspect them due to their distance from County Down. Improvements were thus not pressed forward as strongly as in Down. For twelve years from 1833 Andrews himself urged the tenantry to adopt turnip cultivation and other progressive farming practices, but his efforts met with little enthusiasm. He subsequently relinquished responsibility for these estates to Lanktree, who theoretically was able to devote more time to them.[225] Such an expectation may have been somewhat misplaced, for Lanktree's correspondence with Lady Londonderry reveals that he seldom visited them, and does not appear to have devoted much effort to their improvement.

The Donegal estate in Raymoghy parish was described in the Ordnance Survey Memoir of 1836 as being 'one of the most productive parts of the county'. 'The best land in the parish is near Manorcunningham'. Farm sizes varied from six to sixty acres, the bulk being between twenty and thirty acres. This was corroborated by Andrews, who noted in 1847 that 'the population is small, and the farms comparatively large'.[226] Most farms suffered from a lack of decent fences, making it impossible to grow crops without the constant vigilance of herd boys. There was no cultivation of green crops and little drainage work had been undertaken. The majority of farmers had few domestic comforts or conveniences, and had difficulty making up their rents. The absence of any resident local proprietors or agents to encourage the tenantry was much lamented, and the elimination of rundale and the provision of decent enclosures were seen as the two most urgently needed improvements.[227] The memoir of social life in nineteenth-century Donegal written by the schoolmaster Hugh Dorian, vividly depicts the easy-going lifestyle of the people of the nearby Fanad peninsula, where for many years prior to the famine 'food was in the greatest abundance and easily obtained'. 'Potatoes, the principal food of the people, grew everywhere and to perfection and on any soil into which a spade could be put.' A diet of potatoes, milk and butter was supplemented by fish, which were to be had in abundance. A few weeks' labour in spring and summer raised enough food for a family, with some to spare; and the winters were whiled away attending soirees, dances, balls, wakes, markets, the public house and the shebeen house. Conditioned by years of easy existence, the population, generally speaking, lived from hand-to-mouth, with no thought of a provision made for the future, 'this was the state of people when the potato failure came on the greater part of them'.[228]

This was in strong contrast to other parts of the county, such as Tirhugh, where the establishment by the resident gentry of an active improvement society, together with the efforts of a 'resident and careful agent', had resulted by 1839 in the elimination of rundale and the establishment of properly fenced, regularly shaped farms where improved systems of agriculture were in operation. Such 'improvements' most likely ameliorated the effects of the famine.[229]

According to the Ordnance Survey Memoir for Faughanvale parish, Lord Londonderry's Derry estate was known as the 'ten townlands of Tully'. The average size of holding in the parish was twenty acres, but many were as small as three acres. The farmers around Muff were generally comfortable due to their advanced, albeit incomplete, agricultural knowledge. Green feeding was practiced, usually with turnips. However, there was a total lack of encouragement on every estate, with the exception of those belonging to the London Companies, and the inhabitants of the 'ten townlands of Tully' were the most impoverished of all.[230]

Lord and Lady Londonderry also visited the Derry and Donegal estates in December 1846. The Tully tenantry delivered an address in which, as was customary, they assured Lord Londonderry of their loyalty and devotion to him, and asserted their belief that he would relieve those in want 'in the present trying season'. In his reply, whilst not offering a general abatement of rent, Lord Londonderry noted his decision that all land in Tully under the potato was to be relieved of rent. Furthermore, Lanktree would receive specific instructions for additional aid, if necessary. As in the case of the Antrim estate, he urged the tenants to do their duty in the assurance of his indulgence and kindness.[231] Large reductions in rent were made on smallholdings in Derry, and all potato land in Donegal was also relieved of rent.[232] Despite fierce criticism of his miserliness in *The Londonderry Standard*,[233] Lord Londonderry's policy remained unchanged.[234] In February 1847 Lanktree set out the sums required to carry out necessary drainage work on both estates, but there is no evidence to suggest such work was in fact carried out.[235] Nonetheless, in 1848 Lord Londonderry paid for a supply of guano to the tenantry, and in May 1850 five hundred pounds was spent on providing them with flaxseed and guano, on the understanding, in both cases, that the sums expended would be repaid by the tenants at a future date.[236]

The situation in Tully became critical, and in June 1847 Lanktree reported to Andrews that the tenantry were starving.[237] This is borne out by statistics for the Londonderry workhouse, which in March 1847 was only two short of its full complement of eight hundred inmates. Following additional building work its capacity was increased to eleven hundred, and by December numbers had reached 914, and were almost as high a year later.[238] Nonetheless, in April 1847 Lanktree reported on the favourable appearance and state of cultivation of the Derry and Donegal estates, which was better than any time since the Napoleonic Wars.[239]

The rental of the Derry and Donegal estates in 1845 was £2,373.[240] Like the other Londonderry estates, they were liable for a number of annual fixed charges such as salaries or rent charges for the agent, bailiffs, clergy and schoolmasters; office and estate expenses; crown and chief rents; and county rate and poor rate.[241] In addition they were also responsible for interest on a loan of £18,500 (£738),[242] and annuity payments totalling £220.[243] Rents in Derry and Donegal were not difficult to collect until March 1847,[244] but receipts were subsequently disappointing.[245] In late 1850 Lord Londonderry authorised an abatement of rent on these estates, having seen for himself the difficulties of the tenantry who, unlike their brethren in Down, had 'urged no remonstrance, and relied implicitly on his constant consideration and indulgence'.[246] This effectively wiped out the surplus rental of the estates,[247] and necessitated the Down estates becoming responsible for the interest and annuity payments charged to Derry and Donegal.[248]

The absence of reports by Lanktree's successor, David Cowan, makes it difficult to form a picture of theses estates as they emerged from the famine crisis.

*

The above discussion highlights the differences in the ways in which the famine was experienced in neighbouring counties of Ulster. Such differences may be attributed mainly to the quality of the land and the prevalence of small farmers; the economic state of the tenants on the eve of the famine, and the degree to which they cultivated crops other than the potato; and the availability of additional sources of income. It also highlights the fact that relief policy on the Londonderry estates in Ulster did indeed reflect their individual economic and social circumstances.

In general, Lord Londonderry's policy may be summed up in his words to the Ballymacaldrick tenants 'We must all bow to the will of God; let us try and avert the calamity by renewed exertions of industry on your part, and an anxious desire on ours, to do all in our power to relieve your distresses'. As has been shown, the Londonderrys' powers to offer relief were circumscribed by the financial constraints imposed upon them by a heavy burden of fixed payments, and tempered by the tenants' reluctance to respond to the changing face of agriculture, and learn new techniques, despite substantial support and encouragement to do so. Nonetheless, as Magill notes, 'the Londonderrys did try to respond to the situation with more than fine phrases',[249] the assistance offered reflecting the degree of need. Furthermore, despite mounting arrears, it appears from the agents' correspondence that stringent measures to enforce payment of rent were not implemented until 1850, then being driven in no small measure by Lord Londonderry's annoyance at the support given by his tenantry to the activities of the tenant-right movement, despite the fact that tenant right was acknowledged in its entirety on all his estates.

Lord Londonderry and his agents were convinced that agricultural prosperity in the era of free trade could only be secured by the adoption of improved methods of cultivation and husbandry. Pastoral farming was the way forward. As a result of the repeal of the corn laws, grain supplies were available cheaply from elsewhere, whereas there was a growing home market for meat and dairy products, fuelled by the increasing wealth and expectations of the burgeoning populations of the industrialised towns and cities. In addition, the manure produced by livestock enabled land to be improved and production increased. To survive in the new competitive market, a farm had to be sufficiently large to enable pastoral farming to be practiced; to provide full-time employment for a farmer, assisted by his family as necessary; to generate enough work to justify keeping a pair of horses; to enable a proper rotation to be adopted and sufficient manure produced; and to be flexible enough to adapt to changes in market trends. No longer could there be any expectation of income from alternative sources, such as spinning and weaving, as these activities were becoming increasingly factory-based. Furthermore, in the post-famine period agriculture became steadily more commercialised, encouraged to some extent by the fact that many farming families were coming to expect a more varied diet, including shop-bought goods.[250] Increasingly, tenants no longer thought of their farms as a place to grow sustenance for their families, but more as the means of realising an income from which to purchase such sustenance and provide a better quality of life. One quarter of all farms in Ireland disappeared between 1847 and 1851, the most significant losses occurring in holdings of less than five acres. There was a concomitant increase in the average size of those remaining. In 1845 thirty-four per cent of those holding land had farms of less than five acres, and sixty-six per cent of those holding land held more than that amount. By 1851 twenty per cent of farms were less than five acres and eighty per cent were above five acres.[251] Post-famine Ireland thus became a country of middling farmers.[252]

Lord Londonderry and his agents had no way of predicting that the potato crop would fail repeatedly and the crisis would be so attenuated. Nonetheless, policy on the Londonderry estates from the outset had been to encourage and support turnip husbandry to provide fodder for livestock, from which a farmer could derive income to purchase food and pay his rent, and manure to maintain and enhance the fertility of his land. Their efforts were substantially hindered by the disinclination of the farming community to change, due partly to their innate conservatism, but also to suspicion of the landlords' motives, which many believed to be the encouragement of improvements in order to extract a higher rent.[253] This should not have been a worry to Lord Londonderry's tenants however, where no notice was taken of improvements in the valuation of land.[254] On Lord Londonderry's estates in Down, for certain, not until 1850 was the cultivation of green crops significantly extended and pork beginning to be produced without potatoes.

As elsewhere in Ireland, the ability of farmers on the Londonderry estates to withstand the impact of the repeated failure of the potato crop was governed chiefly by the farmer's dependence on the potato as a source of food for his family and his livestock. Ulster folk had customarily enjoyed a diet which included oatmeal as well as potatoes, but as the population rose from the mid eighteenth century onwards, here, too, an increasing number of families became dependent on the potato. As has been shown, farms on the Londonderry estates in Down and Donegal, and to a lesser extent Derry, were generally speaking larger and more advantageously located than those in Antrim. Proportionally more of the farmers on these estates grew corn as a cash crop, and were making some attempt to grow green crops. By substituting corn for potatoes in their diet they were able to survive, although this strategy, as Andrews remarked, 'diminished the resources available for rent'.[255] However, if by such means they overcame the immediate crisis and went on to adapt their farming practices to the changed circumstances in which they found themselves, they would be able to pay rent in future. They were thus a potential asset rather than a liability to a landlord, who, if wise or wisely advised, would afford them protection and encouragement. It is therefore not surprising that these estates weathered the famine 'storm' best.

As a one commentator noted in February 1847:

> The large farmer is doing well, his produce selling for three times the prices of an ordinary year, his consumption though more costly still very fairly proportioned to his profits. The small farmer is ruined, he must eat his corn, sell his stock at an unseasonable time because he has no fodder and therefore leave himself penniless for the coming year.[256]

It is greatly to their credit that Andrews, Spotswood and Lanktree managed to bring their estates through the famine crisis without being summoned to appear before the Encumbered Estates Court, to which a creditor might apply if the annual charges and interest payments of an estate exceeded half the yearly net income.[257] As Andrews ruefully remarked:

> Nothing is more simple now than a petition to the new summary Encumbered Estates Court, and an ill-natured creditor, in the hands of a gain-seeking attorney, might, without notice or delay, on any morning present such a petition, and destroy the credit of the estate.[258]

Sales under the auspices of the court resulted in an estate coming into the hands of a new landlord under no legal obligation to offer existing tenants compensation for their improvements.[259] The avoidance of this predicament is all the more remarkable when it is remembered that the Down, Magherafelt, Derry and Donegal estates were heavily burdened with fixed annual payments; the Down, Antrim, Derry and Donegal estates were additionally burdened with the costs of constructing and furnishing Mount Stewart and Garron Tower; and the solvency of the Antrim, Derry and Donegal estates was jeopardised by Lanktree's embezzlement of nearly one thousand pounds.

It is interesting to consider why leading tenant-right activists in County Down, such as Guy Stone and John Miller, did not castigate Lord Londonderry for his conduct during the famine. Was it because, as Grant concluded, the crisis in Newtownards was sharp but of short duration, or was it because as intelligent and astute businessmen themselves they appreciated that suffering would necessarily attend the need for change?

The Londonderry estates emerged from the famine crisis leaner, fitter and better able to cope with the changed economic circumstances facing agriculture. This had been achieved by the removal of many bad or inefficient farmers, which was seen by the agents as essential to future well-being and success. As Lanktree said:

> Generally speaking these thinnings were for good. They enlarged some farms – in the hands of better labourers than the emigrants had been – and if many more should go away – of which there is prospect – it will be all the better for the estate – for without the potato crop it is quite impossible for small farmers to live and pay rent especially on poor soils.[260]

As Andrews sagaciously predicted:

> The country has a fearful ordeal to pass through. I still hold to the opinion that the emancipation from mere potato diet would, in the end, of necessity raise the condition of the people, and arrest the fearful multiplication of the population, which has brought matters to their present state, but it must be through change and suffering and trial to all classes that the better state will be attained.[261]

As has been noted, prior to the famine the 3rd Marquess of Londonderry enjoyed a fine reputation as a landlord. This reputation was dealt a blow from which it has never recovered by adverse criticism, particularly in the popular press, of his conduct during the famine and ensuing tenant-right agitation. By reconsidering the Marquess's efforts to relieve distress and hardship on his Irish estates during the famine in the light of his financial position at the time, the response of his tenantry, and the moral philosophy which influenced his actions and those of his agents, this article may permit commentators to form a more accurate, informed and fair judgement of his actions and conduct.

ACKNOWLEDGEMENTS

I am extremely grateful to Trevor Parkhill, Bill Crawford, Annesley Malley and Yvonne Hirst for their help in preparing and sourcing material for this article.

ABBREVIATIONS

Casement: Anne L. Casement, 'The Management of Landed Estates in Ulster in the Mid-Nineteenth Century with Special Reference to the Career of John Andrews as Agent to the 3rd and 4th Marquesses of Londonderry from 1828 to 1863' (unpublished doctoral thesis, Queen's University of Belfast 2002)

DRO: Durham Record Office, Papers of the Marquesses of Londonderry and their Families, Irish Correspondence, D/Lo/C

Kennedy: Liam Kennedy and others, *Mapping the Great Irish Famine: A Survey of the Famine Decades* (Dublin 1999)

Kinealy and Parkhill: Christine Kinealy and Trevor Parkhill (eds), *The Famine in Ulster: the regional impact* (Belfast 1997)

PRONI: Public Record Office of Northern Ireland

PRONI Antrim: Public Record Office of Northern Ireland, The Earl of Antrim Estate Papers, D/2977

PRONI Antrim, Correspondence: Public Record Office of Northern Ireland, The Earl of Antrim Estate Papers, D/2977/5/1/8, Correspondence of Frances Anne Marchioness of Londonderry, 1840–64

PRONI Antrim, Reports: Public Record Office of Northern Ireland, The Earl of Antrim Estate Papers, D/2977/6, Reports of the Estate of the Marchioness of Londonderry

PRONI Castlereagh: Public Record Office of Northern Ireland, The Castlereagh Papers, D/3030/P, Letters and copy letters, mainly from Sir Charles Stewart, to Castlereagh …

PRONI Dawson: Public Record Office of Northern Ireland, Letters of Rt Hon.
George Robert Dawson to William H. Freemantle, T/2603
PRONI Londonderry Estate: Public Record Office of Northern Ireland, The
Londonderry Estate Office Archive, 1629 – c. 1940, D/654

NOTES

1   U.H. Hussey de Burgh, *The Landowners of Ireland. An Alphabetical List of the Owners of Estates of 500 Acres or £500 Valuation and upwards ...* (Dublin 1878) 277.

2   H. Montgomery Hyde, *The Londonderrys: A Family Portrait* (London 1979) 267.

3   U.H. Hussey de Burgh, *The Landowners of Ireland. An Alphabetical List of the Owners of Estates of 500 Acres or £500 Valuation and upwards ...* (Dublin 1878) 277.

4   Casement, 1–2; *Notes relating to the Manor of Sal, explanatory of the Terrier of 1845* (London 1846) 9, which notes that rental was only received on 19,531 acres, the remaining 3,540 acres consisting of freeholds and glebe.

5   J.S. Curl, *The Londonderry Plantation 1609–1914: The History, Architecture, and Planning of the Estates of the City of London and its Livery Companies in Ulster* (Chichester, Sussex 1986) 326.

6   PRONI D/2977/36, Antrim Estate maps; unbound: D/2977/36/7/1, Map of part of the Antrim Estate as entailed upon the Most Honourable Lady Frances Anne Vane now the Marchioness of Londonderry, January 1836. According to PRONI Antrim, Reports: D/2977/6/3, Report on the estates of the Marquis and Marchioness of Londonderry in County Antrim by John Lanktree, 4 September 1844, the Ordnance Survey calculated the acreage to be 10,091 statute acres.

7   H. Montgomery Hyde, *The Londonderrys: A Family Portrait* (London 1979) 19–21, 31–32.

8   Casement, 62–70.

9   Angelique Day and Patrick McWilliams (eds), *Ordnance Survey Memoirs of Ireland Vol. 6: Parishes of County Londonderry 1 1830, 1834, 1836, Arboe, Artrea, Ballinderry, Ballyscullion, Magherafelt, Termoneeny* (Belfast 1990) 91; Casement, 52.

10 Casement, Chapter 3.

11 *Ibid.*, Chapter 5; DRO, D/Lo/C 158 (154), John Andrews to Lord Londonderry, 6 February 1851.

12 i.e. for the Bellaghy estate leased from the Vintners' Company by the Countess Dowager of Clancarty, Lord Strafford and Sir Robert Bateson, and for Mr Dawson's Castledawson estate, see *Report from Her Majesty's Commissioners of Inquiry into the State of the Law and Practice in Respect to the Occupation of Land in Ireland* [605], HC 1845, xix. (earl of Devon, chairman), *Minutes of Evidence*, pt i [606], HC 1845, xix, 653 page loose and unnumbered, 3.

13 David Roberts, *Paternalism in Early Victorian England* (London 1979) 2, 6.

14 *Ibid.*, 4–6.
15 'An Address by the Marquis of Londonderry to the Tenantry of his Down Estates in 1841.', *The Newtownards Chronicle*, 21 October 1911, 8; '15th Annual Meeting of the Newtownards and Comber Farming Society.', *The Times*, 20 October 1841, 6.
16 'To the Editor of the Sentinel.', *The Londonderry Sentinel*, 13 February 1847.
17 DRO, D/Lo/C 512 (41), John Andrews to Lord Castlereagh, 11 December 1847.
18 *Ibid.*, D/Lo/C 512 (17), John Andrews to Lord Londonderry, 14 March 1847.
19 Trevor McCavery, 'The Famine in County Down', in Kinealy and Parkhill, 99–128, 101.
20 Trevor McCavery, *Newtown: A history of Newtownards* (Belfast 1994) 130.
21 R.W. Sturgess, 'The Londonderry Trust, 1819-54', *Archaeologia Aeliana*, X, 5th series (1982) 179–92, 180.
22 *Ibid.*,180–82.
23 Casement, 15, 214–15.
24 Alan Heesom, ' "Not Friends of a Day": The Third Marquess of Londonderry and his County Down Tenants, 1822–1854' (unpublished paper given at 11th Conference of Irish Historians in Britain 4 April 1998) 1–12, 3.
25 PRONI Londonderry Estate, D/654/N, Estate Management: D/654/N1/14, Valuation book of Co. Down Estate, 1851.
26 PRONI, Londonderry Papers, T/1536: T/1536/5, Statistical survey of the Co. Down estate of the Marquess of Londonderry by Maurice Collis, June 1848, Table 5.
27 Angelique Day and Patrick McWilliams (eds), *Ordnance Survey Memoirs of Ireland Vol. 7: Parishes of County Down II 1832–4, 1837, North Down & The Ards* (Belfast 1991) 36, 41.
28 *Report from Her Majesty's Commissioners of Inquiry into the State of the Law and Practice in Respect to the Occupation of Land in Ireland* [605], HC 1845, xix. (earl of Devon, chairman), *Minutes of Evidence*, pt i [606], HC 1845, xix, 544, 5–6, 9; 546, 50–52.
29 PRONI, Londonderry Papers, T/1536: T/1536/5, Statistical survey of the Co. Down estate of the Marquess of Londonderry by Maurice Collis, June 1848, 7.
30 Angelique Day and Patrick McWilliams (eds), *Ordnance Survey Memoirs of Ireland Vol. 7: Parishes of County Down II 1832–4, 1837, North Down & The Ards* (Belfast 1991) 108; Samuel Lewis, *A Topographical Dictionary of Ireland*, 2 vols (London 1837) II, 435.
31 Kennedy, 133 says Down did not participate at all, but James Grant, 'The Great Famine in County Down', in Lindsay Proudfoot (ed.), *Down, History and Society: Interdisciplinary Essays on the History of an Irish County* (Dublin 1997) 353-82, 359 cites instances of such works.
32 James Grant, 'The Great Famine in County Down', in Lindsay Proudfoot (ed.), *Down, History and Society: Interdisciplinary Essays on the History of an Irish County* (Dublin 1997) 353–82, 353–55.
33 DRO, D/Lo/C 512 (21), John Andrews to Lord Londonderry, 14 May 1847.
34 Kennedy, 135.

35   James Grant, 'The Great Famine in County Down', in Lindsay Proudfoot (ed.), *Down, History and Society: Interdisciplinary Essays on the History of an Irish County* (Dublin 1997) 353–82, 368.

36   James S. Donnelly Jnr, 'The Soup Kitchens', in W.E. Vaughan (ed.), *A New History of Ireland, v. Ireland under the Union, I. 1801–70* (Oxford 1989) 307–14, 313.

37   DRO, D/Lo/C 512 (2, 5), John Andrews to Lord Londonderry, 10 January 1847, 18 January 1847.

38   *Ibid.*, D/Lo/C 512 (8), John Andrews to Lord Londonderry, 2 February 1847.

39   *Ibid.*, D/Lo/C 512 (16), John Andrews to Lord Londonderry, 1 March 1847.

40   *Ibid.*, D/Lo/C 512 (17), John Andrews to Lord Londonderry, 14 March 1847.

41   *Ibid.*, D/Lo/C 512 (8), John Andrews to Lord Londonderry, 2 February 1847.

42   'The State of the Poor in the North.', *The Banner of Ulster*, 5 February 1847.

43   'State of the Poor in the North., *The Banner of Ulster*, 26 February 1847.

44   DRO, D/Lo/C 512 (9), John Andrews to Lord Londonderry, 5 February 1847.

45   *Ibid.*, D/Lo/C 512 (18), John Andrews to Lord Londonderry, 21 March 1847.

46   James Grant, 'The Great Famine in County Down', in Lindsay Proudfoot (ed.), *Down, History and Society: Interdisciplinary Essays on the History of an Irish County* (Dublin 1997) 353–82, 374–75.

47   Kennedy, 136; James Grant, 'The Great Famine in County Down', in Lindsay Proudfoot (ed.), *Down, History and Society: Interdisciplinary Essays on the History of an Irish County* (Dublin 1997) 353–82, 376.

48   Trevor McCavery, 'The Famine in County Down', in Kinealy and Parkhill, 99–128, 121.

49   DRO, D/Lo/C 512 (17), John Andrews to Lord Londonderry, 14 March 1847.

50   *Ibid.*, D/Lo/C 512 (18), John Andrews to Lord Londonderry, 21 March 1847.

51   James S. Donnelly Jnr, 'The Administration of Relief, 1847–51', in W.E. Vaughan (ed.), *A New History of Ireland, v. Ireland under the Union, I. 1801–70* (Oxford, 1989) 316–29, 326–27.

52   DRO, D/Lo/C 512 (18), John Andrews to Lord Londonderry, 21 March 1847.

53   Kennedy, 126.

54   DRO, D/Lo/C 512 (36), John Andrews to Lord Londonderry, 1 November 1847.

55   *Ibid.*, D/Lo/C 512 (41), John Andrews to Lord Castlereagh, 11 December 1847.

56   Trevor McCavery, 'The Famine in County Down', in Kinealy and Parkhill, 99–128, 117.

57   PRONI, BG25/A/1, Letter of Resignation from Robert Nicholson to the Poor Law Commissioners, 4 October 1847.

58   DRO, D/Lo/C 512 (41), John Andrews to Lord Castlereagh, 11 December 1847.

59   Kennedy, 137.

60   'The New Poor-Law. – Refusal to Appoint Relieving Officers. – Antrim Union.', *The Belfast News-Letter*, 21 September 1847.

61   Kennedy, 137.

62 DRO, D/Lo/C 512 (21, 23), John Andrews to Lord Londonderry, 14 May 1847, 13 June 1847.
63 *Ibid.*, D/Lo/C 158 (164), John Andrews to Lord Londonderry, 1845–46.
64 PRONI Londonderry Estate, D/654/H, Estate Accounts: D/654/H2/7, Ledger 1828–1850, 183.
65 Casement, 130–32.
66 Lord Londonderry's eldest son and heir to his Irish estates.
67 Casement, 9–11; PRONI Londonderry Estate, D/654/H, Estate Accounts: D/654/H2/7 and H2/8, Ledger 1828-1850 and Ledger 1850–1864; PRONI, The Mark Cassidy Papers, D/1088: D/1088/113, Lord Londonderry, 24 April 1834.
68 PRONI Londonderry Estate, D/654/H, Estate Accounts: D/654/H2/7, Ledger 1828-1850, 74, 165; D/654/H2/8, Ledger 1850–1864, 82–84.
69 Casement, Appendix 2.
70 PRONI Londonderry Estate, D/654/H, Estate Accounts: D/654/H2/7, Ledger 1828-1850, 199, 207, 222, 230, 247; D/654/H2/8, Ledger 1850–1864, 12.
71 DRO, D/Lo/C 512 (17), John Andrews to Lord Londonderry, 14 March 1847.
72 *Ibid.*, D/Lo/C 512 (5, 21), John Andrews to Lord Londonderry, 18 January 1847, 14 May 1847.
73 Trevor McCavery, *Newtown: A history of Newtownards* (Belfast 1994) 129.
74 James Grant, 'The Great Famine in County Down', in Lindsay Proudfoot (ed.), *Down, History and Society: Interdisciplinary Essays on the History of an Irish County* (Dublin 1997) 353–82, 374–75.
75 DRO, D/Lo/C 512 (9, 18), John Andrews to Lord Londonderry, 5 February 1847, 21 March 1847.
76 'The State of the Poor in the North.', *The Banner of Ulster*, 5 February 1847.
77 DRO, D/Lo/C 512 (12), Lord Londonderry to John Andrews, 16 February 1847.
78 *Ibid.*, D/Lo/C 512 (17), John Andrews to Lord Londonderry, 14 March 1847.
79 *Ibid.*, D/Lo/C 512 (21), John Andrews to Lord Londonderry, 14 May 1847.
80 'Rate-In-Aid – Marquis of Londonderry.', *The Downpatrick Recorder,* 14 April 1849, 3.
81 DRO, D/Lo/C 158 (80), John Andrews to Lord Londonderry, 18 July 1850.
82 *Ibid.*, D/Lo/C 512 (29), John Andrews to Lord Londonderry, 4 August 1847.
83 *Ibid.*, D/Lo/C 158 (113), John Andrews to Lord Londonderry, 7 April 1851; Casement, 215.
84 *Ibid.*, D/Lo/C 512 (2), John Andrews to Lord Londonderry, 10 January 1847.
85 *Ibid.*, D/Lo/C 158 (58), John Andrews to Lord Londonderry, 20 January 1850.
86 *Ibid.*, D/Lo/C 158 (102), John Andrews to Lord Londonderry, 7 November 1850.
87 *Ibid.*, D/Lo/C 158 (211), John Andrews to Lord Londonderry, 29 July 1852. See Christine Kinealy, 'Introduction' in Kinealy and Parkhill, 1–14, 1, who gives dates of the famine as 1845–52; and Trevor Parkhill, 'The Famine in County Londonderry', in Kinealy and Parkhill, 147–168, 163, who notes uncertainty surrounding the duration of the famine.
88 DRO, D/Lo/C 158 (159), John Andrews to Lord Londonderry, 26 April 1851.

89 *Ibid.*, D/Lo/C 158 (58), John Andrews to Lord Londonderry, 20 January 1850.
90 *Ibid.*, D/Lo/C 158 (109), John Andrews to Lord Londonderry, 18 December 1850.
91 Casement, 205–06, 208.
92 PRONI Londonderry Estate, D/654/H, Estate Accounts: D/654/H2/7, Ledger 1828–1850, 33, 44; D/654/H2/8 Ledger 1850–1864, 45–46.
93 DRO, D/Lo/C 512 (21), John Andrews to Lord Londonderry, 14 May 1847.
94 Angelique Day and Patrick McWilliams (eds), *Ordnance Survey Memoirs of Ireland Vol. 7: Parishes of County Down II 1832–4, 1837, North Down & The Ards* (Belfast 1991) 44.
95 DRO, D/Lo/C 158 (160), Circular to the Tenantry, 29 November 1851.
96 'Lord Londonderry and his Tenants.', *The Downpatrick Recorder*, 28 November 1846, 4.
97 DRO, D/Lo/C 512 (21), John Andrews to Lord Londonderry, 14 May 1847.
98 PRONI, MSS 7320, MIC 9B, Reel 8 1822–1866: Agent's Report 1849.
99 DRO, D/Lo/C 164 (87), Lord Londonderry to Downshire Tenantry, 16 October 1850.
100 DRO, D/Lo/C 158 (160), Circular to the Tenantry, 29 November 1851; Casement, 229–30.
101 DRO, D/Lo/C 158 (80, 102, 159), John Andrews to Lord Londonderry, 18 July 1850, 7 November 1850, 26 April 1851.
102 Casement, 132.
103 Newtownards initially £100 and £20 from Lady Londonderry, see DRO D/Lo/C 512 (15), John Andrews to ?Lord Castlereagh, 21 February 1847; Comber £10 per month, see 'State of the Poor in the North.', *The Banner of Ulster*, 26 February 1847.
104 Cahal Dallat, 'The Famine in County Antrim', in Kinealy and Parkhill, 15–34, 27; Paul Magill, *Garron Tower, County Antrim* (Belfast 1990) 35.
105 'To the Editor of the Londonderry Standard.', *The Londonderry Standard*, 22 January 1847.
106 'Over 70 Years Ago. The Marquis of Londonderry's Down Estates. Mr John Andrews, Agent, Addresses the Tenantry.', *The Newtownards Chronicle*, 14 October 1911, 8.
107 'Lord Londonderry and his Tenants.', *The Downpatrick Recorder*, 28 November 1846, 4.
108 DRO, D/Lo/C 158 (60, 62), John Andrews to Lord Londonderry, 10, 18 February 1850.
109 *Ibid.*, D/Lo/C 512 (32), John Andrews to Lord Londonderry, 21 August 1847.
110 Sidney Andrews, *Nine Generations – A History of the Andrews Family, Millers of Comber*, edited by J. Burls (n.p. 1958) 122.
111 James S. Donnelly Jnr, *The Land and the People of Nineteenth-Century Cork* (London 1975) 187.
112 DRO, D/Lo/C 512 (10), John Andrews to Lord Londonderry, 14 February 1847.
113 'To the Editor of the Sentinel.', *The Londonderry Sentinel*, 13 February 1847.
114 'Over 70 Years Ago. The Marquis of Londonderry's Down Estates. Mr John

Andrews, Agent, Addresses the Tenantry.', *The Newtownards Chronicle*, 14 October 1911, 8.

[115] DRO, D/Lo/C 158 (182), Andrew McCutcheon to Lord Londonderry, 3 February 1852.

[116] 'Correspondence. Tenant Compensation. To William Sharman Crawford, Esq.', *The Belfast Mercury,* 12 January 1853.

[117] F.M.L. Thompson review of W.A. Maguire 1972 and 1974, *Ir. Econ. Soc. Hist.*, 2 (1975) 74–77, 76.

[118] DRO, D/Lo/C 512 (21), John Andrews to Lord Londonderry, 14 May 1847.

[119] *Ibid.*, D/Lo/C 512 (24), John Andrews to Lord Londonderry, 20 June 1847.

[120] *Ibid.*, D/Lo/C 158 (96), John Andrews to Lord Londonderry, 20 October 1850.

[121] *Ibid.*, D/Lo/C 512 (8), John Andrews to Lord Londonderry, 2 February 1847.

[122] PRONI, Londonderry Papers, T/1536: T/1536/5, Statistical survey of the Co. Down estate of the Marquess of Londonderry by Maurice Collis, June 1848, 2.

[123] *Report from Her Majesty's Commissioners of Inquiry into the State of the Law and Practice in Respect to the Occupation of Land in Ireland* [605], HC 1845, xix. (earl of Devon, chairman), *Minutes of Evidence*, pt i [606], HC 1845, xix, 546, 39.

[124] DRO, D/Lo/C 158 (104), John Andrews to Lord Londonderry, 29 November 1850.

[125] 'Entertainment to Lord and Lady Castlereagh, at Newtownards.', *The Downpatrick Recorder*, 28 August 1847, 4.

[126] 'Dinner to the Marquis of Londonderry.', *The Downpatrick Recorder*, 24 November 1855, 2.

[127] PRONI, Londonderry Papers, T/1536: T/1536/5, Statistical survey of the Co. Down estate of the Marquess of Londonderry by Maurice Collis, June 1848.

[128] Oliver MacDonagh, 'The Economy and Society 1830–45', in W.E. Vaughan (ed), *A New History of Ireland, v. Ireland under the Union, I. 1801–70* (Oxford 1989) 218–41, 234.

[129] PRONI, Londonderry Papers, T/1536: T/1536/5, Statistical survey of the Co. Down estate of the Marquess of Londonderry by Maurice Collis, June 1848, 5.

[130] PRONI Londonderry Estate, D/654/N, Estate Management: D/654/N1/14, Valuation book of Co. Down Estate, 1851.

[131] PRONI Antrim, Reports: D/2977/6/3, Report on the estates of the Marquis and Marchioness of Londonderry in County Antrim by John Lanktree, 4 September 1844.

[132] *Ibid.*, D/2977/6/4A, 'Statistical Report' on the Antrim estates of the Marquis and Marchioness of Londonderry for 1845 by John Lanktree, 8 November 1845.

[133] *Ibid.*, D/2977/6/4B, 'Statistical Report' on the Antrim estates of the Marquis and Marchioness of Londonderry for 1847 by John Lanktree, 1 October 1847.

[134] PRONI Antrim, Correspondence: D/2977/5/1/8/8/8, John Lanktree to unnamed gentlemen, 6 March 1847.

[135] PRONI Antrim, Reports: D/2977/6/4A, 'Statistical Report' on the Antrim estates of the Marquis and Marchioness of Londonderry for 1845 by John Lanktree, 8 November 1845.

136 *Ibid.*, D/2977/6/4B, 'Statistical Report' on the Antrim estates of the Marquis and Marchioness of Londonderry for 1847 by John Lanktree, 1 October 1847.

137 *Ibid.*

138 Expects to be repaid for this, at least in part, see PRONI Antrim, Correspondence: D/2977/5/1/8/8/17, 38, John Lanktree to Lady Londonderry, 5 April 1847, 30 September 1847.

139 PRONI Antrim, Reports: D/2977/6/4D, 'Statistical Report' on the Antrim estates of the Marquis and Marchioness of Londonderry for 1848 by John Lanktree, 30 December 1848.

140 Expects to be repaid for this, with interest, see PRONI Antrim, Correspondence: D/2977/5/1/8/8/17, 38, John Lanktree to Lady Londonderry, 5 April 1847, 30 September 1847.

141 To which Lady Londonderry made handsome contributions, see PRONI Antrim, Correspondence: D/2977/5/1/8/8/10–11, John Lanktree to Lady Londonderry, 8 and 14 March 1847.

142 PRONI Antrim, Reports: D/2977/6/4B, 'Statistical Report' on the Antrim estates of the Marquis and Marchioness of Londonderry for 1847 by John Lanktree, 1 October 1847.

143 PRONI Antrim, Correspondence: D/2977/5/1/8/8/5, John Lanktree to Lady Londonderry, 9 February 1847.

144 *Ibid.*, D/2977/5/1/8/8/41, John Lanktree to Lady Londonderry, 29 November 1847.

145 PRONI Antrim, Reports: D/2977/6/4B, 'Statistical Report' on the Antrim estates of the Marquis and Marchioness of Londonderry for 1847 by John Lanktree, 1 October 1847. Here Lanktree being economical with the truth as PRONI Antrim, Correspondence: D/2977/5/1/8/10/1, John Lanktree to Lady Londonderry, 28 February 1848 says the sum collected included payments towards arrears of 1845, and this was achieved only by recourse to the legal measures available to him for the recovery of rent, see *Ibid.*, D/2977/5/1/8/8/36, John Lanktree to Lady Londonderry, 7 September 1847.

146 PRONI Antrim, Correspondence: D/2977/5/1/8/8/28, 38 John Lanktree to Lady Londonderry, 1 June 1847, 30 September 1847.

147 *Ibid.*, D/2977/5/1/8/8/17–18, John Lanktree to Lady Londonderry, 5 and 17 April 1847.

148 DRO, D/Lo/C 512 (32), John Andrews to Lord Londonderry, 21 August 1847.

149 PRONI Antrim, Correspondence: D/2977/5/1/8/8/36, John Lanktree to Lady Londonderry, 7 September 1847.

150 DRO, D/Lo/C 512 (36), John Andrews to Lord Londonderry, 1 November 1847.

151 PRONI Antrim, Correspondence: D/2977/5/1/8/8/21, 36, John Lanktree to Lady Londonderry, 5 May 1847, 7 September 1847.

152 Cahal Dallat, 'The Famine in County Antrim', in Kinealy and Parkhill, 15–34, 24.

153 PRONI Antrim, Correspondence: D/2977/5/1/8/8/2, John Lanktree to Lady Londonderry, 13 January 1847.

154 Jimmy Irvine, 'Lady Frances Anne Vane's County Antrim Estate', *The Glynns*, 3 (1975) 18–26, 21.
155 *Ibid.*, 22.
156 Kennedy, 137.
157 PRONI Antrim, Correspondence: D/2977/5/1/8/10/6, John Lanktree to Lady Londonderry, 16 May 1848.
158 *Ibid.*, D/2977/5/1/8/10/7, 11, John Lanktree to Lady Londonderry, 30 May 1848, n.d.
159 *Ibid.*, D/2977/5/1/8/10/12, John Lanktree to Lady Londonderry, ?11 September 1848.
160 *Ibid.*, D/2977/5/1/8/8/31, John Lanktree to Lady Londonderry, 16 June 1847.
161 PRONI Antrim, Reports: D/2977/6/4D, 'Statistical Report' on the Antrim estates of the Marquis and Marchioness of Londonderry for 1848 by John Lanktree, 30 December 1848.
162 PRONI Antrim, Correspondence: D/2977/5/1/8/11/1, John Lanktree to Lady Londonderry, ?6 January 1849.
163 PRONI Antrim, D/2977/7B, Rentals: D/2977/7B/104, Rental, Marchioness of Londonderry, 1843–1848.
164 PRONI Antrim, Correspondence: D/2977/5/1/8/11/33, John Lanktree Lady Londonderry, 14 November 1849.
165 PRONI Antrim, D/2977/7B, Rentals: D/2977/7B/120, Rental, Marchioness of Londonderry, 1849–1860, 28.
166 PRONI Antrim, Correspondence: D/2977/5/1/8/8/45, ?Londonderry agent at Wynyard to Lord Londonderry, December 1847.
167 PRONI Londonderry Estate, D/654/H, Estate Accounts: D/654/H2/7, Ledger 1828–1850, 24; DRO, D/Lo/C 519 (8), Andrew Spotswood to Lord Londonderry, May 1847.
168 PRONI Antrim, Correspondence: D/2977/5/1/8/8/28, John Lanktree to Lady Londonderry, 1 June 1847; DRO, D/Lo/C 158 (164), John Andrews to Lord Londonderry, 1845–6.
169 DRO, D/Lo/C 158 (154), John Andrews to Lord Londonderry, 6 February 1851.
170 Jimmy Irvine, 'John Lanktree: Londonderry agent in Carnlough, 1843–1850', *The Glynns*, 8 (1980) 51–53, 53; DRO, D/Lo/C 158 (88), John Andrews to Lord Londonderry, 8 September 1850.
171 DRO, D/Lo/C 158 (88), John Andrews to Lord Londonderry, 8 September 1850.
172 PRONI Antrim, Reports: D/2977/6/4A, 'Statistical Report' on the Antrim estates of the Marquis and Marchioness of Londonderry for 1845 by John Lanktree, 8 November 1845; Hector McDonnell, 'The Mad World of Captain Kerr' (unpublished manuscript) 81.
173 PRONI Antrim, Correspondence: D/2977/5/1/8/8/41, John Lanktree to Lady Londonderry, 29 November 1847.
174 Paul Magill, *Garron Tower, County Antrim* (Belfast 1990) 28, 30.
175 PRONI Antrim, D/2977/54/1/1–16, Specifications and estimates for the construction of a tower on Garron Point, Co. Antrim and additional works by

Charles Campbell of Newtownards 1846–50: D/2977/54/1/4, Estimate in detail of Point of Garron Tower first plan for the Marchioness Vane Londonderry, unsigned, n.d.

176 David Cowan was another Londonderry agent who from 1849 had special responsibility for the Derry and Donegal estates, see *The Londonderry Sentinel*, 9 November 1849.

177 DRO, D/Lo/C 158 (109), John Andrews to Lord Londonderry, 18 December 1850.

178 PRONI Antrim, Correspondence: D/2977/5/1/8/10/12, John Lanktree to Lady Londonderry, ?11 September 1848.

179 DRO, D/Lo/C 158 (88), John Andrews to Lord Londonderry, 8 September 1850.

180 PRONI Antrim, D/2977/54/11/1–14, Accounts, estimates and receipts in respect of money paid to Charles Campbell for work at Garron Tower 1850: D/2977/54/11/1, Garron Tower Account no. 1 to 1 March 1850.

181 Paul Magill, *Garron Tower, County Antrim* (Belfast 1990) 25.

182 *Ibid.*, 5.

183 PRONI Antrim, Correspondence: D/2977/5/1/8/8/41, John Lanktree to Lady Londonderry, 29 November 1847.

184 *Ibid.*, D/2977/5/1/8/11/21, John Lanktree to Lady Londonderry, 4 June 1849.

185 Paul Magill, *Garron Tower, County Antrim* (Belfast 1990) 25.

186 Edith, Marchioness of Londonderry, *Frances Anne: The Life and Times of Frances Anne Marchioness of Londonderry and her husband Charles Third Marquess of Londonderry* (London 1958) 248.

187 Angelique Day and Patrick McWilliams (eds), *Ordnance Survey Memoirs of Ireland Vol. 7: Parishes of County Down II 1832–4, 1837, North Down & The Ards* (Belfast 1991) 71–72.

188 Casement, 66.

189 PRONI Antrim, Reports: D/2977/9A–B, Richard Wilson to Lady Londonderry, 26 November 1856.

190 PRONI Londonderry Estate, D/654/H, Estate Accounts: D/654/H2/7, Ledger 1828–1850, 71, 97, 143, 185, 216.

191 *Rental of the Manor of Sal, in the County of Londonderry, for the year 1845* (London 1846) 73.

192 Coleraine, The Honourable the Irish Society, *Report of a Deputation of the Irish Society: 1836*, 76.

193 *Notes relating to the Manor of Sal, explanatory of the Terrier of 1845* (London 1846) 84.

194 Coleraine, The Honourable the Irish Society, *Report of a Deputation of the Irish Society: 1841*, 61.

195 DRO, D/Lo/C 519 (4, 8), Andrew Spotswood to Lord Londonderry, 10 March 1847, May 1847.

196 Samuel Lewis, *A Topographical Dictionary of Ireland*, 2 vols (London 1837) I, 294.

197 Angelique Day and Patrick McWilliams (eds), *Ordnance Survey Memoirs of Ireland Vol. 6: Parishes of County Londonderry 1 1830, 1834, 1836, Arboe,*

Artrea, Ballinderry, Ballyscullion, Magherafelt, Termoneeny (Belfast 1990) 85–87, 90, 95–96, 104.

198 Trevor Parkhill, 'The Famine in County Londonderry', in Kinealy and Parkhill, 147–168, 155.

199 Angelique Day and Patrick McWilliams (eds), *Ordnance Survey Memoirs of Ireland Vol. 6: Parishes of County Londonderry I 1830, 1834, 1836, Arboe, Artrea, Ballinderry, Ballyscullion, Magherafelt, Termoneeny* (Belfast 1990) 96.

200 Trevor Parkhill, 'The Famine in County Londonderry', in Kinealy and Parkhill, 147–168, 153.

201 *Ibid.*, 157.

202 DRO, D/Lo/C 512 (9), John Andrews to Lord Londonderry, 5 February 1847.

203 PRONI Londonderry Estate, D/654/N, Estate Management: D/654/N2/30, Photocopies of 11 letters and papers from Andrew Spotswood, Millbrook, Co. Londonderry to 3rd Marquess of Londonderry relating to accounts for Magherafelt estate; distressed situation of the poor, 1837–1847.

204 Confirmed in Trevor Parkhill, 'The Famine in County Londonderry', in Kinealy and Parkhill, 147–168, 157

205 DRO, D/Lo/C 519 (4), Andrew Spotswood to Lord Londonderry, 10 March 1847.

206 *Ibid.*, D/Lo/C 519 (6), Andrew Spotswood to Lord Londonderry, 19 April 1847.

207 *Ibid.*, D/Lo/C 519 (7), Andrew Spotswood to Lord Londonderry, 17 May 1847.

208 *Ibid.*, D/Lo/C 519 (10), Andrew Spotswood to Lord Londonderry, 22 October 1847.

209 Trevor Parkhill, 'The Famine in County Londonderry', in Kinealy and Parkhill, 147–168, 165.

210 PRONI Dawson, T/2603/1, G.R. Dawson to W.H. Freemantle, 17 January 1847.

211 *Ibid.*

212 *Ibid.*, T/2603/2, G.R. Dawson to W.H. Freemantle, 3 February 1847.

213 DRO, D/Lo/C 519 (6, 8), Andrew Spotswood to Lord Londonderry, 19 April 1847, May 1847.

214 *Ibid.*, D/Lo/C 519 (3), Andrew Spotswood to Lord Londonderry, 5 February 1847.

215 *Ibid.*, D/Lo/C 519 (5, 8), Andrew Spotswood to Lord Londonderry, January and February 1847, May 1847; *Notes relating to the Manor of Sal, explanatory of the Terrier of 1845* (London 1846) 9.

216 PRONI Castlereagh, D/3030/P/145, Letter from Castlereagh, Mount Stewart, to Stewart, about family finances and a proposed new settlement, November 1816; Casement, 21–22; PRONI Londonderry Estate, D/654/E, Trust Deeds: D/654/E3/4, Trust accounts October 1849–June 1850.

217 Casement, 26.

218 PRONI, Salters' Company Irish Estate Records, D/4108, D/4108/4/7/1 description: D/4108/4/7/1/3, Arrears book of the Manor of Sal 1846–1850.

219 DRO, D/Lo/C 519 (5, 8, 9, 11), Andrew Spotswood to Lord Londonderry,

January and February 1847, May 1847, July and August 1847, November 1847.

220 PRONI Dawson, T/2603/3, G.R. Dawson to W.H. Freemantle, 14 November 1847.

221 *Ibid.*, T/2603/8, 9, G.R. Dawson to W.H. Freemantle, 16 June 1848, 26 July 1849.

222 *Ibid.*, T/2603/9, G.R. Dawson to W.H. Freemantle, 26 July 1849.

223 *Ibid.*, T/2603/12, G.R. Dawson to W.H. Freemantle, 26 May 1850.

224 *Ibid.*, T/2603/14, G.R. Dawson to W.H. Freemantle, 11 December 1850.

225 'To the Editor of the Sentinel.', *The Londonderry Sentinel*, 13 February 1847.

226 DRO, D/Lo/C 512 (9), John Andrews to Lord Londonderry, 5 February 1847.

227 Angelique Day and Patrick McWilliams (eds), *Ordnance Survey Memoirs of Ireland Vol. 39: Parishes of County Donegal II 1835-6, Mid, West and South Donegal* (Belfast 1997) 132, 140–41, 143–44.

228 Hugh Dorian, *The Outer Edge of Ulster: A memoir of social life in nineteenth-century Donegal*, edited by Breandan Mac Suibhne and David Dickson (Dublin 2001) 210–14.

229 James Anderson, 'Rundale, Rural Economy and Agrarian Revolution: Tirhugh 1715–1855', in William Nolan, Liam Ronayne and Mairead Dunlevy (eds), *Donegal, History and Society: Interdisciplinary Essays on the History of an Irish County* (Dublin 1995) 447–70, 458–59, 462–63.

230 Angelique Day and Patrick McWilliams (eds), *Ordnance Survey Memoirs of Ireland Vol. 36: Parishes of County Londonderry XIV 1833–4, 1836, 1838, Faughanvale* (Belfast1996) 17–18, 20, 25, 30.

231 'Visit of the Marquis of Londonderry to his Estates in Derry and Donegal.', *The Londonderry Sentinel*, 5 December 1846.

232 'To the Editor of the Sentinel.', *The Londonderry Sentinel*, 13 February 1847.

233 'The Three Marquises.', *The Londonderry Standard*, 8 January 1847. This newspaper, edited by the tenant-right activist James McKnight, espoused the landlord/tenant conflict as a means of maintaining circulation in an increasingly competitive market, see Casement, 236–39.

234 'To the Editor of the Sentinel.', *The Londonderry Sentinel*, 13 February 1847.

235 PRONI Antrim, Correspondence: D/2977/5/1/8/8/7, John Lanktree to Lord Londonderry, 13 February 1847.

236 DRO, D/Lo/C 158 (88), John Andrews to Lord Londonderry, 8 September 1850.

237 *Ibid.*, D/Lo/C 512 (24), John Andrews to Lord Londonderry, 20 June 1847.

238 Trevor Parkhill, 'The Famine in County Londonderry', in Kinealy and Parkhill, 147–168, 157-58.

239 PRONI Antrim, Correspondence: D/2977/5/1/8/8/19, John Lanktree to Lord Londonderry, 25 April 1847.

240 PRONI Londonderry Estate, D/654/H, Estate Accounts: D/654/H2/7, Ledger 1828–1850, 185.

241 DRO, D/Lo/C 158 (164), John Andrews to Lord Londonderry, 1845–46.

242 PRONI Londonderry Estate, D/654/E, Trust Deeds: D/654/E2/27, Covenant to pay interest on loan of £20,000 secured by mortgage of the Derry and

Donegal estates, 16 April 1833; DRO, D/Lo/C 158 (164), John Andrews to Lord Londonderry, 1845–46.

243 i.e. £80 less than £300 stated in DRO, D/Lo/C 158 (164), John Andrews to Lord Londonderry, 1845–46, because from 1844 Down estates were responsible for Lady Blandford's annuity, see Casement, 134.

244 PRONI Antrim, Correspondence: D/2977/5/1/8/8/7, John Lanktree to Lord Londonderry, 13 February 1847.

245 *Ibid.*, D/2977/5/1/8/8/19, John Lanktree to Lord Londonderry, 25 April 1847.

246 DRO, D/Lo/C 164 (87), Lord Londonderry to the Downshire Tenantry, 16 October 1850.

247 PRONI Londonderry Estate, D/654/H, Estate Accounts: D/654/H2/8, Ledger 1850–1864, 82.

248 DRO, D/Lo/C 158 (109), John Andrews to Lord Londonderry, 18 December 1850.

249 Paul Magill, *Garron Tower, County Antrim* (Belfast 1990) 35.

250 Kennedy, 209; Samuel Clark, *Social Origins of the Irish Land War* (Princeton 1979) 125.

251 Kennedy, 162–63, Tables 15 and 16.

252 Alvin Jackson, *Ireland 1798–1998: Politics and War* (Oxford 1999) 82.

253 Jonathan Bell and Mervyn Watson, *Irish Farming: Implements and Techniques, 1750–1900* (Edinburgh 1986) 12.

254 DRO, D/Lo/C 158 (182), Andrew McCutcheon to Lord Londonderry, 3 February 1852.

255 *Ibid.*, D/Lo/C 512 (2), John Andrews to Lord Londonderry, 10 January 1847.

256 Elizabeth Grant, *The Highland Lady in Ireland: Journals 1840–50*, edited by Patricia Pelly & Andrew Tod (Edinburgh 1991) 303.

257 James S. Donnelly Jnr, 'Landlords and Tenants', in W.E. Vaughan (ed.), *A New History of Ireland, V. Ireland under the Union, I. 1801–70* (Oxford 1989) 332–48, 346–47. See also Casement, 133.

258 DRO, D/Lo/C 158 (109), John Andrews to Lord Londonderry, 18 December 1850.

259 Lindsay Proudfoot, 'Encumbered Estates Court', in S.J. Connolly (ed.), *The Oxford Companion to Irish History* (Oxford 1998) 171.

260 PRONI Antrim, Reports: D/2977/6/4D, 'Statistical Report' on the Antrim estates of the Marquis and Marchioness of Londonderry for 1848 by John Lanktree, 30 December 1848.

261 DRO, D/Lo/C 512 (23), John Andrews to Lord Londonderry, 13 June 1847.

Medicine as Cultural Baggage in the Ulster-Scots Settlements of the Valley of Virginia

KENNETH W. KELLER

A MERICAN HISTORIANS have given us many studies of Ulster-Scot or, as they have been more commonly called, 'Scotch-Irish' settlements in the United States and the careers of their clergy, attorneys, journalists, and writers. Students of the folkways of the regions of the American backcountry where they and their descendants lived have also focused upon such topics as their language, architecture, family structure, child rearing, religion, death customs, foods, dress, use of leisure time, wealth, and political ideas have received attention.[1] When studies of the American Ulster-Scots do mention health, medicine, and disease, it is usually to call attention to the Ulster-Scots or Scottish 'influence' upon or 'contribution' to American medicine, rather than to describe and explain medical practices in the Ulster-Scots settlements.[2] One centre of Ulster-Scots settlement that produced considerable medical activity was the principal Ulster-Scot settlement in Virginia, called since the eighteenth century 'the Irish Tract', the area spanning Augusta and Rockbridge counties and comprising the Upper James River Valley and the Upper Shenandoah River Valley between the Blue Ridge Mountains on the east and the first ridge of the Appalachians. In the Irish Tract, many customs involving health, disease, and medicine were similar to or borrowed from the homeland in Ulster, even long after the first of the Ulster-Scots families settled there. This medical culture, part of the cultural baggage of the American Ulster-Scots, persisted there long after it was losing favour elsewhere.

Although most emigrants to the New World insisted that living conditions there were more healthful than in the old country, especially since upland areas like the Valley of Virginia suffered from fewer of the fevers commonly associated with coastal areas and seaports, there was nevertheless much opportunity for the practice of various healing arts in the new settlements.[3] In the Irish Tract of the Valley of Virginia, at least three parallel medical traditions emerged between the middle of the eighteenth century and the 1840s–50s. Domestic medicine was the first, usually practised by self-educated healers in the home in the absence of a professionally trained physician. Domestic healers relied largely upon native herbs and the potions, infusions, decoctions, salves and ointments that could be made from them. Most domestic healers were women, especially mothers, who practised their art when access to a professional physician was either unavailable or too expensive. Midwives also were adept at domestic medicine.

A second form of healing was professional medicine, applied only by professionally-trained physicians and based in part on herbs, but also upon the use of minerals and so-called 'heroic' methods of treatment that aggressively interfered with body processes to effect a cure. The final form of treating the body was the early counterpart of alternative medicine, taking to so-called 'medicinal' waters. A variety of wells and springs in western Virginia attracted large numbers of patients and physicians who believed that taking these waters would produce health-giving benefits for the body. All three of these approaches to medicine were based upon specific theories and cultural attitudes toward health, related to approaches to healing common in the north of Ireland, and experiencing a process of refinement in the nineteenth century.[4] The healers and the patients of the Irish Tract all confronted treatment of disease within these limits.

Although the healers and their approaches to healing found in the Irish Tract used different methods to treat disease, each was a product of its own time and culture, and whatever cultural baggage recent settlers in the American backcountry had brought with them. They knew of the Scottish Enlightenment, which brought with it assumptions about medicine and healing that domestic, professional, and alternative healers of the Irish Tract all shared. To them, disease was a problem of the individual, so it had to be treated by careful diagnosis and administration of medication. Each human illness could be understood by noting its symptoms and treatment of each patient using means whose purported effectiveness had been observed in the treatment of other individuals. The healers of the Irish Tract wanted to apply a 'common sense' approach to treatment. One needed to observe, diagnose and administer whatever medications seemed to work. Among these healers magic cure-alls, incantations, and sorcery were disregarded, but there was also little thought of prevention, scientific experimentation, keeping of biological statistics, cellular biology, epidemiology, or sepsis. Each human system was thought to be in balance in normal conditions, and when the components of the system became imbalanced, it was the job of the healer to put the system back into equilibrium. Observers understood that the blood circulated and that human anatomy was comprised of interconnected systems, but there was little understanding of chemical processes. The discovery of bacteria and viruses and much modern physiology and chemistry were decades in the future.[5]

Of the three forms of healthways known in the Irish Tract, by far the form of medicine most commonly used was domestic medicine, which was usually applied in the home by women who provided primary care for family members or by self-taught clergymen who administered medicine to their parishioners. Students of the Ulster-Scots settlements in North America can see several treatments similar to those back home. Whether the treatments were coincidentally similar or direct borrowings from Ulster remains uncertain; nevertheless, many domestic remedies used the same plant materials to treat the same symptoms. It was also true that many of the remedies used were unique to the American environment.

One practitioner of domestic medicine was Anne Montgomery Lewis Peyton (1802–50), the great-grand-daughter of John Lewis, one of the earliest Ulster-Scot settlers on the Irish Tract.[6] She dispensed treatment to a large family and its slaves at the family plantation at Montgomery Hall, near Staunton in the Irish Tract. In Great Britain and Ireland, among the most commonly used domestic medications were garlic, onion (often roasted), dandelion, flaxseed, chamomile, horehound, plantain, tansy, and bark from the elm tree.[7] In treating members of her household for coughs and colds, Ms Peyton used horehound, which was also used in County Cavan for coughs, heartburn, and rheumatism. Dandelion, a plant that was not native to North America, migrated to the New World with its first settlers; Ms Peyton employed it as a tonic, which was also a use it had in Britain and Ireland. She also prepared a tonic of tansy, which also was done in the land of her ancestors. Several of her preparations, however, were purely American in their origins, because the plants upon which they were based were found only in North America. Dogwood, used for a tonic, the Balm of Gilead tree, used for 'dyspepsia', and wild cherry for coughs and colds, were American applications.[8]

Clergyman and physician Joseph Doddridge (1769–1826), writing about medicine in the settlements of western Virginia, found that pucoon or blood-root, which is not a plant found in the British Isles, was used as a vomit in western Virginia settlements. Bowman root, Indian meal, and ipecac were American preparations that were not based on European flora, but were used in the backcountry settlements of the Ulster-Scots.[9] He also reported on the use of bark of elm for burns, garlic for inflammation of the trachea or larynx, and walnut bark for either purges or vomits; all of these applications were familiar in Britain and Ireland.[10] The local historian John Lewis Peyton (1824–96), son of Anne Montgomery Lewis Peyton, noted the use of maple sugar, another uniquely American product, among the early Ulster-Scots settlers to treat coughs.[11] If these samplings are representative, by the late eighteenth century, the Ulster-Scots residents of the Irish Tract were well along the way to developing a hybrid folk medical culture that borrowed from both their ancestral environment and that of the New World.

The disease environment of the Irish Tract was similar to that of Ulster with a few exceptions. From wherever they moved in America, emigrants from Ulster usually assured their relatives in correspondence they were able to send back home that their new surroundings were healthier than those to which they had been accustomed; of course this also generally applied to the conditions they had just endured on board ship or in crowded coastal seaports. Since the Valley of Virginia around the Irish Tract was 1,200–1,500 feet above sea level, the collection of symptoms for various diseases people of the eighteenth and nineteenth centuries called 'fevers', dysentery, and typhus of the seacoast and crowded seaports were rare in the Irish Tract. The communities in which the emigrants settled were dispersed settlements, with individual farmsteads scattered about the landscape, so the chances of some contagion spreading would be lessened. Most health problems known to the settlers of the Valley of Virginia were also common in Ulster. By the 1850s the most important common killer among them was consumption, and the numerous remedies that were supposed to treat coughs, colds, pleurisy, and croup[12] indicate that respiratory diseases were widespread. The designation 'consumption' included a multitude of illnesses and did not necessarily signify tuberculosis.[13] Respiratory ailments would be especially likely to occur in closed, smoky cabins and damp stone houses in the winter. Domestic treatments for illnesses classed as consumption included wild cherry, garlic, and preparations of various syrups. Other common ailments involved worms in children and burns from open hearth fires; these too would have been familiar to emigrants from the north of Ireland. One problem of the day unknown in Ireland was snakebite, and most recollections of domestic medicine included extensive remedies for treating it involving chestnut bark, gunpowder and salt, white plantain, and walnut fern.[14] Whatever the ailment, and regardless of the inexpertise of the practitioner, the popular remedies of domestic medicine survived long into the twentieth century among the descendants of the Ulster-Scots in the southern uplands.[15]

By the time of the early nineteenth century, the crude treatments of domestic medicine had undergone refinement, perhaps linked to the increased circulation of newspapers and manuals in backcountry settlements like the Irish Tract. Like the mixtures administered by housewives, patent medicines and the advice delivered in newspapers and self-help medical books were substitutes for official medicine delivered by professional physicians, although the books and preparations were often the work of men who displayed professional medical credentials. The male purveyors of these supposed remedies presumed that their compounds and therapies were superior to the crude ministrations of housewives.[16]

The competition with domestic medicine began with settled town life in the Irish Tract. In 1787, almost as soon as a newspaper began publication in the Valley of Virginia, advertisements appeared in it for patent medicines. In subsequent years, merchants routinely advertised the arrival of their 'spring goods' from cities like Philadelphia and Baltimore, and included in these were drugs. The newspaper of Lexington, in the Irish Tract, printed various simple remedies for bowels, ringworm, shingles, corns, warts, burns, and scalds as well as uses for cork and the common nettle.[17] In 1836 the *Staunton Spectator* revealed that iodine might be used to treat consumption, that holly could work in curing fever, even in cases where Peruvian or Jesuit's bark – quinine – failed, and that creosote was an effective treatment for toothache.[18] Mother's preparations from local plants were no longer sufficient; exotic chemicals and imports from the tropics were more effective.

Newspapers also published advertisements addressed to patients that suffered from specific problems, such as 'dyspepsia', or medications like 'stomachic bitters' or 'vegetable nervous cordial' that specifically addressed these ailments.[19] By the 1830s, road transportation to the Irish Tract from cities had improved sufficiently so that more patent medicines could be sold in general merchandise stores. Such products as spirits of turpentine, Rowland's macassa oil, chlorine tooth wash, lump or calcined magnesia, and Peters' bilious pills for the liver were on merchants' shelves in Staunton and nearby Waynesboro. The Staunton merchant Edmund Berkeley advertised that he sold 'every article in the drug line', with dozens of preparations from Boston, New York, and Philadelphia markets.[20] Many of these concoctions, such as Dr McLane's worm specific, were specifically for children, to expel worms, to purge the body, and to curb a fever.[21] Male physicians, asserting their professional training, were challenging maternal control of domestic medicine.

Books published by well-known physicians began to appear to provide advice for medicine in the home. As early as 1796, a copy of William Buchan's *Domestic Medicine: or, the Family Physician* was in the Irish Tract's Library of Liberty Hall Academy, the predecessor institution of Washington and Lee University.[22] Buchan's *Domestic*

Medicine was widely used for many years afterwards in America. At the beginning of the nineteenth century, Staunton newspapers also advertised popular health books such as John Theobald's 1734 *Everyman His Own Physician* and Gardner's advice book on the gout.[23] One Staunton resident lost his copy of James Ewell's *Medical Companion,* probably the most commonly used book of home medical advice in Virginia.[24] In nearby Fincastle, south of the Irish Tract in Botetourt County, Virginia, Ralph Schenck published in 1842 *The Family Physician,* a work plagiarised from Ewell in many parts. Schenck was also used in western Virginia and in the library of the Franklin Society of Lexington, a subscription library and debating society that existed from 1813 to the late nineteenth century.[25]

By the 1830s and 1840s, other similar medical books by professionally trained physicians that recommended proper remedies found their way to the book collection of the Franklin Society, which acquired works such as Jacob Bigelow's *American Medical Botany,* a book that identified native American plants and their uses.[26] Both James Ewell and Ralph Schenck's works contained not only remedies, but also pious observations and moral advice for families, which otherwise might have come from a housewife.[27] They cited with great respect the leading medical authorities from overseas, especially from the University of Edinburgh.

Male physicians who challenged folk medicine in the Irish Tract represented the second form of medicine practised there between the mid eighteenth and the first half of the nineteenth century. They were trained professionals, most of them having studied in Scotland or in the new American medical schools that had been founded since the mid eighteenth century. Not all the physicians of the Irish Tract were of Ulster descent, but most were and, accordingly, they served as a channel for bringing professional medical standards as practised in Ulster and in Scotland to the United States. These followers of the Edinburgh school of medicine brought with them to the Irish Tract the theories about human physiology and anatomy, the origins of disease, and the proper *materia medica* for treatment of illness. They attempted to establish institutions for the education of physicians and to create a medical 'profession' with its own standards and ethics. In this way they helped to transplant an aspect of Ulster-Scot culture to the United States.

As had been the case with Reformed Protestantism, or the developing commercial trading network of the eighteenth century, the medical culture of the professional Ulster-Scot physicians in America transcended the geographic and cultural limitations of northern Ireland and spread to the New World. It was not their creation, but they were its transmitters. By the late eighteenth century the University of Edinburgh was the leading medical school in Western Europe, and its faculty and students' medical authority was widely respected. Unlike universities in England, its doors were opened to dissenting Protestants, so from all over Europe non-Anglican Protestants seeking an education could matriculate there without discrimination. Because the doors were open to non-Anglicans, dissenters like the Presbyterians interested in medical study flocked there, even after American independence. Its students, like the physician-statesman Benjamin Rush of Philadelphia, in turn taught others. In this relatively tolerant setting, its faculty and those of other Scots universities were centres of the Scottish Enlightenment.[28]

The medical ideas of the Scottish Enlightenment were the principal contribution of the physicians of the Irish Tract to the medical environment of western Virginia. Physicians who adhered to the assumptions of this eighteenth century flowering of scientific and philosophical thought all sought a single theory upon which a system of medicine might be based. Through the teaching of the eminent professor of medicine William Cullen (1710–90) and his students, like John Brown (1735–88) and William Buchan (1729–1805), these professional physicians employed a system of observation, description, analysis, and therapy they considered to be rational or scientific, in that it was not based on earlier doctrines linked to astrology, signatures, correspondences, old wives' tales, folk remedies, or divine intervention, but rather upon a supposedly 'common sense' case-by-case method of analysis. Although Cullen and his disciples may have differed on precisely the system that best explained human health and disease, they all assumed that the healthy body was in some sort of equilibrium, and that when this equilibrium was out of balance, it was necessary to apply techniques to put the organs of the back into alignment. The physician of the time usually achieved 'balance' by various methods of adding to or depleting bodily fluids, usually through purges, emetics, laxatives, tonics, diuretics, expectorants, cathartics, blood-letting, or drugs that made people sweat, called diaphoretics.[29] Edinburgh theorists differed over whether the blood vessels, nerves, or other tissues were where this balance was to be achieved, but generally they used blood-letting and other aggressive treatments. Most of these treatments would be entirely repudiated today, except by some purveyors of so-called 'alternative medicine', but nevertheless in one way or another, this approach was at the core of professional medicine in America at least until the 1820s, and not completely rejected until the mid nineteenth century, and was in the forefront of the attack on traditional domestic medicine as it had been practised before the coming of professional physicians to the American backcountry. American physicians and readers of medical advice books like those of William Buchan, Ralph Schenck, and James Ewell continued to encounter these authorities' advice well after the American Civil War.

The leading physicians of the Irish Tract had studied at Edinburgh or in medical schools in America whose faculties themselves were trained by the theorists of Edinburgh. Foremost among them were Alexander Humphreys of Staunton and his students Ephraim McDowell and Samuel Brown.[30] Other physicians in Augusta County, which surrounded Staunton, included Addison Waddell, George C. McIntosh, William McCue, William R. Blair, John McChesney, J. Lewis and John McChesney. In Lexington were Samuel L. Campbell, James McDowell, and Archibald Graham. William Alexander Carruthers practised in Lexington while indulging in literary pursuits.[31] Some Irish Tract physicians of the late eighteenth and early nineteenth centuries like Alexander Humphreys had been born in Ulster and had then studied in Edinburgh under such eminent medical authorities as William Cullen. Others like Ephraim McDowell and Samuel Brown were born in America, but went to complete their medical education at Edinburgh. Others were graduates of the two great Philadelphia medical schools, those of the University of Pennsylvania, on whose faculty served Benjamin Rush, and the Jefferson Medical

College. These American-trained physicians then went on to train other American physicians in Virginia and the Ohio Valley like Joseph Nash McDowell, whose career took him to the Mississippi Valley city of St. Louis, where he opened a medical college of his own. Many Virginians attended medical school at Penn, all of whose early faculty had themselves studied at Edinburgh.[32] From Edinburgh and Philadelphia a succession c. medical practitioners spread across North America.

Since Edinburgh and Edinburgh-derived medical education had such a grip on the way American physicians in the Irish Tract were trained, the remedies favoured among Edinburgh practitioners were widely employed in the Irish Tract and, at least among some of them, they were employed well after they had gone out of favour elsewhere. A surviving apothecary's register from Staunton from the late eighteenth century shows the use of methods and prescriptions such physicians and the people wealthy enough to afford them preferred. Over 300 lay people of Staunton and vicinity purchased medications from the apothecary between 1787 and 1790. The list of medications sold reveals that the apothecary's customers had a wide variety of drug preparations available to them, many of them coming from overseas and that the medical theories of Edinburgh were well employed in the Irish Tract.

One of the most frequent patrons of the Staunton apothecary was the Edinburgh-trained physician Alexander Humphreys. He purchased the emetics tartar and ipecacuahna, the antispasmodics camphor and niter, the cathartics jalap, Glauber's salts, fruit of tamarind, and magnesia; the evacuants (used to expel worms) colichum, ammonium salts, infusion of senna, Dover's powder, and syrups of squills and spigel root; the laxative glycerin; astringent of galls; the diuretic copaiba; the stimulant sage; and the diaphoretic and evacuant guaiacum. Besides using many medications that were supposed to deplete the body of its fluids, Humphreys used various sedatives and narcotics as well as various compounds of mercury. Unlike the herbal preparations used in domestic medicine, the professionally trained physicians like Humphreys used metals, including arsenic, silver, lead and antimony for an emetic. Other physicians of the Irish Tract whose notes survive administered blood-letting, opiates, quinine, cupping, blistering, and vaccination.[33] Medications of the late eighteenth century were still in used on the eve of the American Civil War, and medical faculty at the University of Pennsylvania continued to feature them in their publications on *materia medica*.[34]

Medicine as practised by professionally trained physicians in the Irish Tract remained orthodox and conventional, and their scientific interests did not range far into new approaches to treatment. Some indication of the scientific or medical concerns of the Irish Tract's physicians can be seen in the reading tastes of doctors. Early nineteenth century laymen and physicians borrowed many works on phrenology, the craze begun in the 1830s that attempted to analyse character by studying the shape of the head. Other medical works consulted were Benjamin Rush's essays, especially his essay on the mind, and Andrew Combe's 1835 *Principles of Physiology Applied to the Preservation of Health*, Robert Burton's psychological treatise of 1851 *The Anatomy of Melancholy*, and the 1841 study of *Human Physiology* by Robley Dunglison, professor of medicine at the University of Virginia. By the 1850s Lexington medical readers were studying Martyn Paine's *Medical and Physiological Commentaries*. This selection of readings would not have challenged many of the basic assumptions about diagnosis and treatment that the Irish Tract physicians applied. It was not until after 1869 that the Franklin Society began to acquire works by French clinicians, whose medical authority began to surpass that of the Edinburgh school in the 1830s.[35]

Since the trained physicians were in competition with folk medical traditions, physicians responded by developing a sense that they were, indeed, professionals who based their work and reputation upon a code of professional standards, that they alone were the legitimate authorities to consult for the administration of medical procedures, and that they had important responsibilities for public health. There was much popular scepticism about doctoring in both America and in the old country, and newspapers occasionally printed comical descriptions of physicians or their education.[36] However physicians of the Irish Tract referred to themselves as members of a dignified profession, and most outsiders perceived them as such.[37] At times their sensitivity about their professional reputations led to litigation, as it did when Alexander Humphreys sued a local Staunton innkeeper for implying that Humphreys was responsible for the disappearance of an English traveller whose corpse it was alleged ended up on the doctor's dissecting table.[38] Less notoriously, the Irish tract physicians served local government by certifying the qualifications of midwives and by examining applicants for military pensions to verify their claims for compensation.[39] They also were called upon by the state to serve as primitive public health officials. In 1814 the General Assembly of Virginia passed a law for the free distribution of vaccine matter in the event of a smallpox outbreak. In 1822 physicians of the Irish Tract formed a 'Vaccination Institute' to distribute vaccine.[40] After reports of smallpox cases in Baltimore and North Carolina, in 1837 the justices of the Augusta County Court, denying that there was any smallpox in Staunton, noted that there had been one case in the town of Greenville to the south. They called a meeting at the county courthouse in Staunton to recommend the vaccination of everyone in the county and appointed three prominent physicians to serve as vaccine agents to distribute vaccine to county physicians. They also urged the establishment of hospitals for smallpox cases in houses, and called on all practising physicians in the county to vaccinate as many people as they could.[41]

Physicians also attempted to refine and improve their professional status by submitting papers to medical journals and by providing for medical education. Someone in Philadelphia, the medical capital of the early United States as well as its political capital, thought sufficiently well of the physicians of the Irish Tract so that a notice addressed to the medical profession appeared in the *Lexington Intelligencer* in 1823 soliciting articles for the Philadelphia *American Medical Recorder*, a national medical periodical.[42] Irish Tract physicians J. Alexander Waddell of Staunton and S. Kennerly of Augusta County published case reports in the 1854 volume of the *Stethoscope*, a new medical periodical from Richmond.[43] In Staunton, Alexander Humphreys had taken as students a number of aspiring physicians, who dissected cadavers in a structure he called his 'elaboratory'.[44] By 1826 there was sufficient interest in the study of medicine in the Valley of Virginia so that the Virginia legislature chartered the 'College of Physicians of the

Valley of Virginia at Winchester', Virginia's first medical college. The College was ninety miles north of the Irish Tract and too far away for any Irish Tract physicians to participate in it directly, but its creation shows a growing *espirit de corps* among western Virginia doctors.[45]

Some healers of the Irish Tract espoused a third approach to medicine in the late eighteenth and early nineteenth century. They rejected the use of medicines based on metals, especially calomel, a compound of mercury, and heroic methods of restoring equilibrium like blood-letting, cupping, and blistering. One school of dissenters was the Thomsonians, who followed the teachings of a New England physician who advised herbal preparations, enemas, and baths in mineral springs. The Thomsonians, laymen who were not professionally trained and who scorned the use of calomel and blood-letting, were to become a medical craze in America in the 1830s. The Franklin Society of Lexington did receive *The Thomsonian*, a periodical promoting the treatments this medical sect favoured. At least one Thomsonian practitioner worked near Lexington in 1836, where, although he was initially sceptical of Thomsonian ideas as 'Yankee medicine', he maintained that he had cured patients with asthma, paralysis below the hips, fainting, dyspepsia, and rheumatism.[46] Occasionally a local newspaper would advertise remedies like Dr William Evans's medicine for dyspepsia while attacking treatment with calomel by 'mercurial murderers'.[47] More common in the Irish Tract, however, was resort to health springs whose waters patients were to drink or in which they were supposed to bathe. The promotion of the water cure was a popular cause in the Irish Tract, and the area became a place of concourse for people seeking to take to the waters. Going to healing wells and springs was an ancient practice, certainly one familiar to persons from northern Ireland and England, and the springs of western Virginia were well known as sources of healing waters.[48] In the late eighteenth century, in the summer settlers in the Irish Tract would visit the springs near their home, gather after harvest was over, build huts, stable their horses, bathe in the waters, and picnic.[49] Through the early nineteenth century these places became resorts that promised not only medical help, but also opportunity for refined society to display its charms.[50]

Although the springs became centres for social display, they were also supposed to provide medicinal relief for various medical problems. The waters of each spring had specific chemical properties and physical results on the human body, and proprietors of these places were quick to see the profits that could be made by developing bathing houses and inns adjacent to the waters. In 1808 a spring was discovered near Staunton on the plantation of Captain John Bowyer. It was purported to have sudorific, cathartic, and diuretic properties, and the owners made plans to build a bathing house for summer guests.[51] Other spring resorts developed at Stribling Springs in Augusta County, and Wilson or Strickler Springs, Rockbridge Baths, Rockbridge Alum Springs, and Cold Sulphur Springs near Lexington. Some of the springs became the property of descendants of the first Ulster-Scot settlers of the Irish Tract as the waters were discovered on land their ancestors had owned. Most well known of these were Warm Springs and Sweet Springs, whose developers were William and John Lewis, descendants of the Ulster-Scot founder of Staunton, John Lewis. According to one traveler, Sweet Springs was 'the most ancient and celebrated watering-place in this state'.[52] Other Ulster-Scot proprietors included James Caldwell, founder of the White Sulphur Springs resort, and William Erskine and Isaac Caruthers, who established Salt Sulphur Springs in 1821. The latter spa boasted 28 new cabins, a dining and ballroom, six lodging rooms, and stables, and offered its patrons relief from bilious and pulmonary complaints, troubles of the alimentary canal, hemorrhages of the breast, gastric afflictions, gout, and diseases of the bowels using water that contained 'great medicinal powers ... superior to any pharmaceutical preparation.' Promoters of other springs made claims equally as bold. Physicians also purchased the springs and attempted to develop curative resorts, as did the developer of Hot Springs, Dr Thomas Goode, a medical graduate of Pennsylvania and Edinburgh.[53] During the nineteenth century, the literature discussing the medical advantages of various springs expanded and fashionable persons from the eastern and southern United States flocked to the springs. The traffic to the springs brought much unaccustomed excitement to the towns of the Irish Tract.[54] Proprietors of the springs replaced the crude huts and arbors of the eighteenth century with elaborate hotels and reputable physicians who claimed expertise in use of the healing waters. A process of refinement was underway in the springs of Virginia.

The medical theories that physicians used to justify resort to the springs, though different in small details from the conventional practice of physicians in the heyday of the springs, were still generally based on the theories of official medicine of the day. Most of the literature of the springs near the Irish Tract supported their use with accepted 'heroic' principles of the Edinburgh school and with typical treatments that physicians educated there would have used. According to leading advocates of the Virginia springs, the most important result of drinking the waters was to purge the body of its 'gross humours' and 'unloading and cleansing the machinery of the body'.[55] Such treatment, according to John J. Moorman, M.D., was useful for opthalmia, rheumatism, slight affections of the skin, chronic inflammation of the liver, chronic inflammation of the rectum, and obstructions of the kidneys and glands. Advocates of the springs regarded the use of the waters as alternatives to, not replacements for, mercury.[56] Dr Samuel Goode, proprietor of the Hot Springs, continued to administer grains of calomel during the 1830s to patients with liver complaints who came to the springs for relief even as the use of this mercury compound was coming under attack. Dr A.A. Campbell used calomel at the Hot Springs in 1838 to treat himself for bilious colic. Another sufferer combined drinking sulphur water, sweat baths, and generous administrations of the diuretic dandelion to cure what he believed was a liver disorder. Sufferers visiting the White Sulphur Springs reported taking the 'blue mass', possibly a compound of mercury related to the ubiquitous 'blue pills', to relieve liver complaints. A patient at Salt Sulphur Springs reported that he took its water, the blue pill, and blistering successfully to treat a haemorrhaging liver.[57] The treatments of the Virginia springs, like the medical practices of the Irish tract from the mid eighteenth century to the antebellum years, did not change.

What explains the conservative character of medicine in the Irish Tract before the Civil War? The Irish Tract, though on an important artery of transportation to the West, was not a generator or receiver of new ideas. Innovations in treatment came from elsewhere, usually the North, and new approaches like Thomsonianism were regarded as

Yankee medicine. More importantly, the physicians of the Tract carried with their cultural baggage a respect for the teachings of Edinburgh, which was not merely a school of medicine influential among the Ulster-Scots, but dominated the medicine of western society until it was replaced by French and German authority. The Irish Tract physicians consulted medical books based on Edinburgh assumptions and trained at schools like that of Pennsylvania with many ties to the professors of Edinburgh. Not only sentiment and nostalgia tied them to the theories of Edinburgh, and not merely a disposition to conservative practices, but also the power of Edinburgh's authority in Ulster and in America gave its approach to medicine a long life in the Irish Tract. As the refinement of life in the Virginia backcountry took place, the authority of the medical profession and the reputation of its approach to the healing arts made Edinburgh theories the ossified orthodoxy of antebellum practice in the Irish Tract.

NOTES

1   See especially David Hackett Fischer, *Albion's Seed – Four British Folkways in America* (New York: Oxford University Press, 1989), 605–782, 812–816. Also Grady McWhiney, *Cracker Culture – Celtic Ways in the Old South* (Tuscaloosa, Alabama: The University of Alabama Press, 1988).

2   William C. Lehmann, *Scottish & Scotch-Irish Contributions to Early American Life and Culture* (Washington, D.C.: Lehmann-Spohr, 1980), 65–83; Hugh H. Trout, 'The "Scotch-Irish" of the Valley of Virginia, and Their Influence on Medical Progress in America,' *Annals of Medical History*, n.s., (January 1938) x, 71–82; xi, 162–168; James Thomas Flexner, *Doctors on Horseback—Seven Pioneers of American Medicine* (New York: Collier Books, 1962), 123–158.

3   Fischer, 639.

4   Richard L. Bushman, *The Refinement of America – Persons, Houses, Cities* (New York: Random House, 1992), 61–69, 239–241, 281, 290–306, 390–398, 409–413, 474–5, 480.

5   Lester S. King, *The Medical World of the Eighteenth Century* (Chicago: The University of Chicago Press, 1958); *Transformations in American Medicine – from Benjamin Rush to William Osler* (Baltimore: The Johns Hopkins University Press, 1991), 1–35; Kay K. Moss, *Southern Folk Medicine – 1750–1820* (Columbia, South Carolina: The University of South Carolina Press, 1999), 219–225.

6   Irvin Frazier, comp. *The Family of John Lewis, Pioneer* (San Antonio, Texas: Fisher Publishing Company, 1985) 79, 200–201; [John Lewis Peyton], *Memoir of the Life of John Howe Peyton, in Sketches by His Contemporaries* ... (Staunton, Virginia: A.A. Blackburn & Co., 1894), 257.

7   See articles on each medication in Gabrielle Hatfield, *Encyclopedia of Folk Medicine – Old World and New World Traditions* (Santa Barbara, California: ABC-CLIO, 2004). Patrick Logan, *Irish Country Cures* (New York: Sterling Publishing Co., Inc., 1994), mentions Irish use of garlic and onion for respiratory cures, a use to which they were applied in western Virginia. See 22, 24. Logan also found that dandelion was used for urinary diseases; it was also used for this purpose in America (37–38). Doreen McBride, *What They Did with Plants—A Link with Ireland's Past* (Banbridge, Northern Ireland: Adair Press, 1991), reported that people in Ulster used dandelion as a diuretic and garlic as a cure-all, but especially for stomach upsets and rheumatism. No other plants found in surviving records of the Irish Tract appear in her survey of plants in northern Irish medicine.

8   Hatfield, 203; Beatrice Maloney, 'Traditional Herbal Cures in County Cavan,' (*Ulster Folklife*, Vol. 18 1972) 71.

9   Danielle Lopes, Joan Moser, and Annie Louise Perkinson, *Appalachian Folk Medicine: Native Plants and Healing Traditions* (Warren Wilson College Press, 1997), 18, 26.

10   Joseph Doddridge, *Notes on the Settlement and Indian Wars of the Western Parts of Virginia and Pennsylvania from the year 1763 until the year 1783 inclusive together with a View of the State of Society and Manners of the First Settlers of that Country* (Harrisonburg, Virginia: C.J. Carrier Company, 1981), 272–275. Beatrice Maloney found elm bark used for burns in County Cavan and Ulster people used garlic for a variety of respiratory complaints. See Maloney, 71–73.

11   J.[ohn] Lewis Peyton, *History of Augusta County, Virginia* (Harrisonburg, Virginia: C.J. Carrier, 1983), 47.

12   In the United States, croup meant inflammation of the trachea or larynx.

13   Todd Savitt, *Medicine and Slavery – the Diseases and Health Care of Blacks in Antebellum Virginia* (Urbana, Illinois: The University of Illinois Press, 1981), 110–149. Savitt's figures are calculated from the Federal Census of Mortality for the 1850s.

14   Doddridge, 272; Peyton, *History*, 46. See also Susan M. Palliser, [typescript] 'The Use of Plants in English Folk Medicine, 1600 to 1800' Leeds Folklore Group Monographs in Folk Life Studies No. 1 (Leeds, England: Leeds Folklore Group, School of English, University of Leeds, 1984), which discusses English remedies for snakebite, 39–41. None of these was mentioned in accounts of snakebite treatments in western Virginia.

15   See John C. Campbell, *The Southern Highlander and His Homeland* (Lexington, Kentucky: The University Press of Kentucky, 1921), 205. Campbell reported meeting an old man in the mountains who told him of 24 different herbal teas,

many of which were made from the same plants used in the eighteenth and
early nineteenth century in the Irish Tract.

16 Not until 1811 did an American woman publish a health manual. See Kathleen
Brown, in 'The Maternal Physician – Teaching American Mothers to Put the
Baby in the Bathwater,' in Charles E. Rosenberg, ed., *Right Living – An Anglo-
American Tradition of Self-Help Medicine and Hygiene* (Baltimore, Maryland:
The Johns Hopkins University Press, 2003), 88. On the male physicians' assault
on domestic medicine, see Lamar Riley Murphy, *Enter the Physician – The
Transformation of Domestic Medicine, 1760–1860, 1–100.*

17 [Winchester] *Virginia Gazette,* 11 July 1787; 12 June 1790; 17 September
1791; *Lexington Intelligencer,* 6 February, 4, 30 September 1825.

18 *Staunton Spectator,* 19 January; 1 September 1836.

19 *Staunton Spectator,* 9 February 1837.

20 *Staunton Spectator,* 21 September; 23 November 1837; 29 March 1838.

21 *Staunton Spectator,* 10 May 1838.

22 *Liberty Hall Academy* (Lexington, Virginia: Washington and Lee University,
1999), 65.

23 By 1767 John Theobald's *Everyman His Own Physician* had appeared in ten editions. American editions had been published in Boston, Philadelphia, and
Hartford by 1800. See Murphy 72 and [Staunton] *Political Mirror,* 5 May
1801.

24 James Ewell, *The Medical Companion, or Family Physician, treating of the diseases
of the United States, with their symptoms, causes, cure, and means of prevention:
common cases in surgery, as fractures, dislocations, &c the management and diseases
of women and children. A dispensatory for preparing family medicines,and a glossary
explaining technical terms. To which are added, a brief anatomy and physiology of
the human body, showing, on natural principles, the cause and cure of diseases: an
essay on hygiene, or the art of preserving health without the aid of medicine: An
American materia medica, pointing out the virtures and doses of our medicinal
plants. Also, the nurse's guide* (Philadelphia: Thomas, Cowperthwait & Co.,
1847). J.F. Patterson placed the advert for the lost book in the *Staunton
Spectator,* 12 December 1837. According to the issue of the same newspaper of
5 September 1839, he opened a store to sell drugs, medicines, paints, dyestuffs,
and groceries. His store advertisement boasted that he sold 'Fresh Medicines.'
James Patterson and Edmund Berkeley were competitors in selling medicines in
Staunton. Berkeley also practiced medicine. See *Staunton Spectator,* 15 April
1841.

25 Oren F. Morton, *History of Rockbridge County Virginia* (Baltimore: Genealogical
Publishing Company, 2002), 214–216.

26 The library of the Franklin Society of Lexington was deposited at Washington
and Lee University when the Society went out of existence in 1891. By the end
of the nineteenth century, the collection contained thousands of books, nearly
100 of which are devoted to medicine. The circulation records of the library
have survived, and from them it is possible to see that one of the most

frequently borrowed medical books in the collection in the early nineteenth century was Harvard professor Jacob Bigelow's *American Medical Botany* (1817–20).

27 Ralph Schenck, *The Family Physician, Treating of the Diseases which assault the human system at different periods of life, with their symptoms, causes, and cure. To which are prefixed a treatise on chemistry, shewing the chemical action of bodies on each other. A brief Anatomy and Physiology, shewing the structure and functions of the human body. And a materia medica, pointing out the Virtues and Doses of the Medicines for Family use.* (Fincastle, Virginia: Oliver Callaghan & William W.E. Word, 1842).

28 John D. Comrie, *History of Scottish Medicine to 1800* (London: Balliere, Tindall and Coxe, 1927), 199–253; Douglas Sloan, *The Scottish Enlightenment and the American College Ideal* (New York: Columbia University Press, 1971), 1–35; Oscar Riess, *Medicine in Colonial America* (Lanham, Maryland: University Press of America, 2000), 161–168, 185–187, 233–238, 254–257. 267–416.

29 John Harley Warner, *The Therapeutic Perspective – Medical Practice, Knowledge, and Identity in America, 1820–1885* (Princeton, New Jersey: Princeton University Press, 1997), 23, 40, 46–47; King, 143; Arturo Castiglioni, *A History of Medicine* (New York: Alfred A. Knopf, 1941), 585–586.

30 Richard P. Bell, 'Alexander Humphreys, M.D. – 1757–1802,' *Augusta Historical Bulletin*, Vol. 3, No.2 (Fall 1967), 15–22.

31 Joseph A. Waddell, *Annals of Augusta County, Virginia, from 1726 to 1871.* Second Edition. (Harrisonburg, Virginia: C.J. Carrier Company, 1986), 373–4, 401, 410, 439; Peyton, *History,* 315; Andrew C. Holman, 'Gentlemen, Irregulars, and Eclectics: Who Practised Medicine in Nineteenth-Century Rockbridge County, Virginia?' *Proceedings of the Rockbridge Historical Society*, XII (1995–2002): 45–61; Flexner, 141.

32 George W. Corner, *Two Centuries of Medicine – A History of the School of Medicine, University of Pennsylvania* (Philadelphia: J.B. Lippincott, 1965), 7, 15–57; Lisa Rosner, 'Thistle on the Delaware: Edinburgh Medical Education and Philadelphia Practice, 1800–1825,' *Social History of Medicine: Journal of the Society for the Social History of Medicine* (1992), Vol. 5: 19–42. The *Staunton Spectator* of 15 April 1841 noted that 44 of the medical graduates of the University of Pennsylvania were from Virginia.

33 William R. Blair microfilm Misc. Reel 365, ms. account book, 1837–43, Virginia State Archives, Library of Virginia; John Addison Waddell Records, 1841–1847; 1853–1874, (Joseph K. Ruebush Collection), Business Records Collection, Library of Virginia, Richmond, Virginia.

34 See Apothecary Ledger, 1785–95, from Augusta County, Business Records Collection, Virginia State Archives, Richmond, Virginia. I have used my copy of a materia medica text used at the University of Pennsylvania in 1864 to identify the uses of these medications. See Alfred Stillé, *Therapeutics and Materia Medica. A Systematic Treatise on the Action and Uses of Medicinal Agents Including Their Description and History* (Philadelphia: Blanchard and Lea,1864).

35 I have studied more than 500 pages of the circulation records of the Franklin Society from 1813 to 1866. Hundreds of Lexington residents belonged to the Society, including most of the town's physicians. The circulation records of the Society are contained in the Librarian's Books of the Franklin Society, 1813–1866, in the James Graham Leyburn Library Special Collections, Washington and Lee University, Lexington, Virginia.

36 See 'How to Maake [sic] a Scotch Doctor,' copied from the *Edinburgh Review* in the *Lexington Intelligencer*, 27 July 1826. The Franklin Society of Lexington subscribed to the *Edinburgh Review*, and it was frequently borrowed by Lexington residents. See also the letter of 'C.R.P.******' in the [Fincastle] *Herald of the Valley*, 3 September 1821and 'AMATOR RAPRIETAS' in the same paper 17 September 1821.

37 See Archibald Graham [?] manuscript physician's obstetrical case notes, 1830s–1844, entry of 6 May 1830, Special Collections Department, James Graham Leyburn Library, Washington and Lee University, Lexington, Virginia; [Fincastle] *Herald of the Valley*, 27 August 1821.

38 [Winchester] *Virginia Gazette*, 25 June, 30 July, 20, 27 August, 8 October 1788; Augusta County Court, Office Judgments, Microfilm Reel 69, 20 August 1789, Library of Virginia, Richmond, Virginia; Lyman Chalkley, *Chronicles of the Scotch-Irish Settlement in Virginia, extracted from the original Court Records of Augusta County, 1745–1800* (Baltimore, Maryland: Genealogical Publishing Company), Vol. 1, 391, 404, 508–509.

39 Chalkley, Vol. 3, p. 184, J.T. McAllister, *Virginia Militia in the Revolutionary War* (Hot Springs, Virginia, 1913), 101–6, 109–122, 124–126, 142, 152.

40 [Fincastle] *Herald of the Valley*, 25 February, 3 August 1822.

41 *Staunton Spectator*, 19, 26 January 1837.

42 *Lexington Intelligencer*, 24 May 1823.

43 J. Alexander Waddell, 'Supra Pubic Puncture of the Bladder for Retention of Urine,' and S.Kennerly, 'A Case of Quadruple Birth,' *Stethoscope*, Vol. 4 (1854): 516, 573–574.

44 See Trout.

45 Commonwealth of Virginia, *Acts Passed at a General Assembly of the Commonwealth of Virginia* ... (Richmond, Virginia: Thomas Ritchie, 1826), 82–84. The College had a difficult early history, and was absorbed into the Medical College of Virginia in 1854. See also the *Lexington Intelligencer*, 6 January 1826.

46 See 'The Way I Became a Thomsonian,' *Thomsonian Recorder*, Vol. 5, No. 110 (11 February 1837): 148–149.

47 *Staunton Spectator*, 22 November 1838.

48 Patrick Logan, *Irish Country Cures* (New York: Sterling Publishing Co., 1994), 135–147.

49 Morton, 158–160.

50 Charlene M. Boyer Lewis, *Ladies and Gentlemen on Display – Planter Society at*

the *Virginia Springs, 1790–1860* (Charlottesville, Virginia: The University Press of Virginia, 2001), 57–98.

51 *Staunton Censor*, 20 July 1808.

52 *First Resorts – A Visit to Virginia's Springs* (Richmond, Virginia: Virginia Historical Society, 1987), 6.

53 Lewis, 37; *Lexington Intelligencer*, 4 September 1824; Stan Cohen, *Historic Springs of the Virginias – A Pictorial History*. Revised Edition. (Charleston, West Virginia: Pictorial Histories Publishing Company, 1997), 1–132.

54 *Staunton Spectator*, 22 June 1853.

55 John J. Moorman, *The Virginia Springs with their analysis; and some remarks on their character, together with a directory for the use of the white sulphur water, and an account of the diseases to which it is applicable* (Philadelphia: Lindsay and Blakiston, 1847), 31–33.

56 Moorman, 43.

57 William Burke, *The Mineral Springs of Western Virginia: with remarks on their use and the diseases for which they are* applicable (New York: Wiley and Putnam, 1842), 78; Thomas Goode, *The Invalid's Guide to the Virginia Hot Springs: containing an account of the medical properties of these waters with cases illustrative of their effects* (Richmond, Virginia: P.D. Bernard, 1846), 16, 22, 31–32, 39.

From the North of Ireland to the North River of the Shenandoah

James and Margaret Ramsey, an Ulster-Scot Farming Family in Augusta County, Virginia, c. 1741–1778

LEE K. RAMSEY

FROM THE VICISSITUDES of the agrarian, plantation life in Ulster, came a young couple to colonial America, to face the uncertainties of a new world. Having endured the hardships of their journey at sea, the steady traffic of ships plying the Delaware River must have been a welcome sight. As this new land reflected in their eager eyes and their hopes were rekindled for a new way of life, they would soon make their way into the Virginia Valley, lying between the beautiful Blue Ridge and Appalachian Mountains, to the pioneer settlement of Augusta County, Virginia, most likely under the guidance and indentureship of John Smith, a well known captain of the Augusta County militia and a lesser known promoter of emigrants from the north of Ireland.

The Ramsey family's early history reveals a traditional 'Scotch-Irish' heritage, with the familiar migration and settlement patterns following the 'Old Wagon Road' from Philadelphia, Pennsylvania, crossing the Susquehanna River down into the Shenandoah Valley of Virginia; and, by 1769, the trek made by their children to the North Carolina Piedmont and the Yadkin River Valley region to the Catawba Valley in Mecklenburg County, North Carolina; and, by 1803, they would follow the trails to Tennessee.

Family tradition coupled with current genealogical research has shown the American progenitor of this Ramsey family to be James Ramsay, an Ulster-Scot, and his wife, Margaret, who were among the first generation settlers of Augusta County, Virginia. Their county of origin in the northern province of Ulster is unknown.

The earliest known family records were found in 1976, in the possession of Richard E. Davis, a kinsman and founding president of the Gibson County Tennessee Historical Society. These records came down through the family of John Wesley Ramsey (1840–1901) and his daughter, Lula Virginia (Ramsey) McGee of Gibson County, Tennessee. This early family history states that William Ramsey Sr was born in Pennsylvania about 1740–42, several months after his parents reached America from the north of Ireland; that William Ramsey married Agnes Maria Boyd, who was born in Ireland in 1744, and being five years old when her parents came to American; William and Agnes Maria (Boyd) Ramsey settled in Mecklenburg County, North Carolina, and about 1803, removed to Rutherford County, Tennessee. Included within these early records were the children of William and Agnes Maria (Boyd) Ramsey and their early descendants.

EMIGRATION AND SETTLEMENT

The traditional emigration date of 1740–42, for James and Margaret Ramsay's transatlantic voyage to America, indicates a close correlation between their emigration and the conditions in Ireland which could only have served to see emigration as an escape. These included rising rents for the tenant farmer, the desire to become land owners and the want of economic opportunity, the winter of 1739–40 proving especially harsh, with failing crops, the slump of the linen trade and soaring food prices.[1] The winter of 1739–40 was known in Ulster as 'the time of the black frost,' due to the unusually dark appearance of the ice and because the sun seldom shone during its continuance.[2] In September of 1740, the *Pennsylvania Gazette* ran an advertisement for the ship master of the *Mary Ann* from Belfast. The ship had arrived in Philadelphia with 'a parcel of likely Men and Women servants' and a 'great Variety of White and Check linens'. The following spring, more ships from Ireland loaded with servants landed in Philadelphia.[3]

Unlike previous emigrants these men and women did not have the necessary funds to pay their transport fares. For most emigrants this would amount to nearly a year's wages in Ireland. How James and Margaret Ramsay secured their passage to America is not known, but their modest circumstances as a farming family, coupled with the economic conditions in Ireland, suggest they would have indentured themselves in the service for the usual three or four year term for their passage; after which, James would qualify as a 'yeoman' (freehold farmer). It would be some eleven years plus before Daniel Smith conveyed the North River land to James Ramsey by a deed of 'lease and release' which, as on an Ulster estate lease, created a landlord-tenant relationship between Daniel Smith and James Ramsey; but, upon the completion of the terms of the lease and release instrument, the North River property was transferred to James Ramsey, the same as a land deed conveyance. This eighty acre tract on the North River of the Shenandoah became the Ramsey's American ancestral home. Later, the Ramsey's farmstead and that area along the North River settlement of Augusta County, Virginia was taken into Rockingham County, Virginia with its formation in 1778.

James and Margaret Ramsay established their first homestead on the land of Daniel and Jean Smith, with their 80 acres situated 'on the South Bank of the North River of Shanado'. The date of record for James Ramsay's receiving title to this land was 18 August 1756, and being adjacent to John Davis and John Divir, opposite the mouth of Bear Creek. This land deed is the first record found for James Ramsay, and the first record known in which the traditional Scottish 'Ramsay' surname spelling is used.[4]

Daniel Smith, who deeded the 80 acre tract to James Ramsay, was one of five sons of Captain John Smith of Augusta Co., VA. The Smith family also came from Ireland by way of Philadelphia prior to the arrival of James and Margaret Ramsay. After an initial settlement in Pennsylvania, John Smith appeared before the Orange County, VA court on 26 June 1740, to prove his importation in order to take up public land.[5] With the formation of Augusta County, Virginia in 1745, the Smith's land became a part of this newly created frontier, Virginia county, which became a stronghold for Ulster-Scot settlers.

It is not known where the Ramsey and Smith families became acquainted, but the records reflect a standing relationship of support and trust, whereby James and Margaret Ramsay were able to establish their homestead in order to gain title to their land at a later date. The Revolutionary War pension claims file for their son, James Ramsey, shows that, upon James Ramsey's second tour in the Augusta Co., VA militia, he joined the service as a substitute, in the place of Benjamin Smith,[6] son of Abraham Smith.[7] After the death of the father, James Ramsey, Abraham Smith, a brother of Daniel Smith,[8] along with John Davis, gave bond with Margaret Ramsey, as the administratrix of James Ramsey's estate on 19 November 1760.[9] James Ramsey died intestate in 1760, Augusta County, Virginia, leaving a widow and four children.[10]

THE FIRST FAMILY

1 CHILDREN OF JAMES AND MARGARET RAMSEY:

1 William Ramsey, Sr., b. PA, c. 1740–42;[11] d. Rutherford Co., TN, after 3 Oct. 1831;[12] m. Augusta Co., VA, before 12 Nov. 1767,[13] Agnes/Nancy Maria Boyd, b. Ireland, 1744;[14] d. Rutherford Co., TN, c. 1830;[15] daughter of Robert Boyd, a weaver from Ireland.

2 Unknown child; probably a daughter, who was living with her siblings and their widowed mother on 20 Nov. 1761, Augusta Co., VA.[16]

3 Margaret/Peggy Ramsey, b. North River Settlement, Augusta Co., VA, c. 1748; d. Rutherford Co., TN after Apr., 1813; m. David Rogers of Mecklenburg Co., NC; d. Rutherford Co., TN, 1813.[17]

4 James Ramsey, b. North River Settlement, Augusta Co., VA, 15 Apr 1753;[18] d. Rutherford Co., TN, c. 1848; m. probably Rockingham Co., VA or Mecklenburg, Co., NC, after 1783; his wife's name is unknown; served as a Revolutionary soldier in the Augusta Co., VA militia and the Virginia Continental Army until the close of the war.[19]

AN ULSTER-SCOT FARMING FAMILY

The Augusta County, VA, court records provide a glimpse into the heritage and lifestyle of James and Margaret Ramsey as an Ulster-Scot farming family. Much like their forbearers in Ireland and Scotland they farmed and raised cattle along with the required horses. It appears that James Ramsey had a successful growth of stock at the time of his death in 1760. The inventory of his estate reveals that James had several breed of cattle and several horses:

> One black pacing horse, one sorrel mare, one bay mare, and
> one small black horse;
> One pied (black and white) cow, one brown cow, one black
> cow, one small brown cow, one small red cow, one small bull,
> twelve 2 year old heifers, a two year old heifer listed separately,
> a one year old steer, one small year old heifer and six calves.[20]

Among the farm equipment and tools inventoried were:

> One man's saddle, two small pots of pot hooks, iron and steel,
> two hew and mall rings, one sheaving knife & three reap
> hooks, one felling ax, one jointer, one bell and colter shear and
> plow tacklings.[21]

Also listed in the estate were the following household items: one yard of broad cloth, two and a half yards shalloon,[22] one body coat, one bed and furniture, one spinning wheel, three pewter pots and one dozen spoons.[23]

From David Crockett's autobiography written between 1805–10, he described his wife's use of the spinning wheel as follows: 'My wife had a good wheel, and knowed exactly how to use it. She was also a good weaver, as most of the Irish are, whether men or women, and being very industrious with her wheel, she had in a little or no time, a fine web of cloth, ready to make up ...'.[24]

James and Margaret Ramsey represent the single-family farmstead, which the Scotch-Irish preferred; and which sustained their spirit of individuality, the importance of family and their self-sufficiency.[25] The most common type of settlement in seventeenth and eighteenth century Ulster was the 'clachan', described as a small community of joint tenants who shared the land.[26] James and Margaret brought to the wilderness a heritage of mixed farming in which both crops and livestock were raised.

James Ramsey's list of farm equipment inventoried in his estate reveals farming on a large scale, with the use of the colter shear[27] and plow tacklings.[28] Plow farming required land clearing, as opposed to the hoe cultivation around remaining tree stumps. Many pioneer farmers adopted the slash-and-burn technique from the Indians for clearing farmland.[29] The three reap hooks and a sheaving knife reveal the harvesting of grains – wheat, oats, barley and Indian corn were the dominant crops; also grown were small crops such as flax and cotton for house use.[30] From the growth of James' livestock, it appears that he would have used a portion of the heifers for their value in the meat trade.

Livestock were allowed to graze on land which was not fenced for crops, but usually they remained in the woods.[31] The majority of strays found in Augusta County were heifers or steers.[32] Stray livestock were required to be reported to the county clerk to be recorded in the estray book with the animal's description and value, a procedure which was based on the Tudor English law adopted by Virginia in 1656, to help prevent the abuse or use of stray livestock.[33]

As first generation settlers in Augusta County, Virginia, James and Margaret Ramsey established a self-sufficient and productive farmstead. The tools and household implements inventoried in James Ramsey's estate reflect the skills they brought with them from the north of Ireland. The harvesting of grain or hay was a laborious process, requiring several men from sunrise to sunset to cut one and a half to two acres in one day, and often being assisted by the women.[34] The domestic economy of the household centred around Margaret whose duties were at once onerous and unending – baking, cooking, washing, sewing, milking the cow and churning the butter; she picked, dyed, and carded the wool, broke and carded the flax, spun and wove the cloth, and made the family wardrobe; and raised the children.[35]

In closing the pioneer life of James and Margaret Ramsey in Augusta County, Virginia, the following provides a description of a typical frontier home:

The early log cabins had only one room, with a loft above.

Sometimes the loft was reached by a ladder from the outside, but generally by pins driven in the wall ... inside of the cabin. The door was hung on wooden hinges and ... often made double, one above and one below ... the upper part could ... open to admit light, while the lower part was closed against weather and intruding animals ... The single window was usually covered with oiled paper, admitting a dull ... light. [a] chimney made of stones, straw, sticks and clay completed the cabin.[36]

SOME GENEALOGICAL CORNERSTONES

During the post-Revolutionary War era the Commonwealth of Virginia continued to use the legal principles founded on English common law as applied to land ownership. The underlying principle was the protection of property rights. Land and its improvements became the primary legacy. Among early legal concepts sprang the rule of primogeniture whereby the eldest son inherited his father's land as 'heir at law.' When the father died without a will the rule of primogeniture took effect. The 'heir at law' principle as applied to genealogy produced the axiom 'land is the purest form of relationship.' Land deeds and related documents can provide cornerstones upon which family relationships can be established as well as revealing valuable secondary evidence.

Upon the death of James Ramsey in Augusta Co., VA, in 1760, his eldest son, William Ramsey, inherited his father's 80 acre tract. Prior to William and Agnes Ramsey's removal to Mecklenburg Co., NC, with Agnes's brother, John Boyd, they conveyed their 120 acre tract and the father's 80 acre tract to their mother, Margaret Ramsey.[37]

THIS INDENTURE made the twelfth day of November in the year of our Lord one Thousand seven hundred and sixty seven Between William Ramsey and Agnis his wife of the County of Augusta and Colony of Virginia and Eldest son and Heir in Son to his Father James Ramsey of the one part and Margaret Ramsey of the said County and Colony of the other part ... two tracts or parcels of land ... on the North River of Shanando the one containing one hundred & twenty acres ... being the land that was conveyed ... Ramsey by Silas Hart ... bearing date the fourth & fifth days of June one Thousand seven

Hundred and sixty four The other Containing Eighty acres being the Land that was Conveyed by Daniel & Jane Smith to James Ramsey father of the said William Ramsey ...[38]

Another important concept for land deed genealogy is the 'widow's tract'. In common law, after the death of the husband, the widow during her natural life had use of one-third of all her husband's real estate, and included the last dwelling house. If during the husband and wife's lifetime they decided to sell the land, it was required of the wife to relinquish her dower right[39] to the land in order to provide a clear title. Deeding the two tracts, by William and Agnes Ramsey, to Margaret Ramsey in 1767, gave her ownership and use of all the land with her remaining children; and also became an investment for William and Nancy Ramsey as the land would revert back to them at Margaret's death. Margaret, for whom no other record has been found, probably died in Augusta Co., VA, before the formation of Rockingham Co., VA, in 1778.

With the marriage of William Ramsey and Agnes/Nancy Boyd in Augusta Co., VA,[40] the first family alliance was formed, an alliance which would take them to Mecklenburg Co., NC. There, Nancy and John's father, Robert Boyd, had taken up land on the waters of Long Creek in 1759, while still Anson Co., NC.[41] Robert Boyd relocated to the North River Settlement of Augusta Co., VA,[42] no doubt due to the escalating Indian-settler conflicts in that region of North Carolina's Western frontier. Historian Robert W. Ramsey describes their circumstances as follows: 'Peace on the frontier did not last long. Late in 1758, urged on by the French, the Cherokees resumed their attacks upon the settlers. John and William Ireland, Andrew Morrison, and John Oliphant were among the inhabitants of the Catawba Valley who were 'forced from their lands.' The following year the Indians killed Robert Gillespie and the fourteen-year-old son of Richard Lewis. They then attacked Fort Dobbs, but without success."[43]

William and Nancy Ramsey Sr did not dispose of their two tracts of land in Augusta Co., VA, land until long after their final migration and settlement, which took them from Mecklenburg Co., NC, to Rutherford Co., TN, by 1803. From the court minute records of

Rutherford Co., TN, there is found the following record for William
and Nancy Ramsey dated 23 June 1820, deeding the old Augusta
County land, which became a part of Rockingham Co., VA, in 1778.
Note the 'Ramsay' spelling by this clerk of the court.

> Deed – William Ramsay and Nancy Ramsay of this County to Isaac
> Myers of Rockingham County in the state of Virginia for a tract of
> one hundred and twenty acres & one other tract of Eighty acres both
> lying in said County of Rockingham was deposed in court and there-
> upon the said William Ramsay acknowledged the due execution of
> said deed and therefore the court proceeds to take the female exami-
> nation of said Nancy Ramsay who saith she does freely and of her own
> accord execute the said deed wherefore it is Ordered that the land be
> so Certified.[44]

The execution of the Rockingham Co., VA, deed was witnessed by
Blakeman Colman, Clerk of the Court of Pleas and Quarterly Sessions
of Rutherford County, TN. This deed was executed on 22 June 1820,
and was recorded in Rockingham Co., VA, on 19 February 1821. The
following is a partial abstract of a photocopy of the deed.

> This indenture made and executed the 22 day of June in the Year of
> our Lord 1820 By & between William Ramsey & Nancy Ramsey his
> wife formerly Nancy Boyd Of the first part & Isaac Myers of
> Rockingham County – state of Virginia of the Other part Witnesseth
> that the said William & Nancy his wife in consideration of the sum
> Twelve hundred and fifty – Dollars to them paid at or before the seal-
> ing & delivery of these presents ... the following tracts of land lying in
> the county of Rockingham of Virginia on the North side of the
> Shenandoah River, one of said tracts of Land containing one hundred
> & twenty acres ... South of a small meadow called the Elk Draft near
> Hugh Dever's corner to Silas Hart and Hugh Deaver's lines ... The
> other tract of land containing eighty acres be(ing) the same more or
> less ... Corner to Charles Davis ... the same two tracts or parcels of
> land which descended to the said William Ramsey at the death of his
> father James Ramsey.[45]

READING BETWEEN THE LINES

Also within the records secondary clues may be found which can provide supporting evidence to substantiate and supplement family history traditions. Secondary clues are uncovered within the historical and legal framework of the primary records.

The first record found for William Ramsey Sr provides supporting evidence for his traditional 1740–42 date of birth. William Ramsey Sr's first record of land entry is dated 5 June 1764, Augusta Co., VA, wherein he purchased 120 acres from Silas and Jane Hart.[46] The legal requirement for transacting conveyances or land lease deeds was to be a male having reached the age of majority of twenty-one years, establishing William Ramsey's birth before 5 June 1743. Additional supporting evidence is found within the record for Widow Ramsey with her four children dated 20 November 1761,[47] showing that no child had had reached the age of majority at that date. It may also be regarded as additional supporting evidence for James and Margaret Ramsay's emigration period during the Ulster sailing seasons of 1740–42. William Ramsey's birth, after his parent's arrival to Pennsylvania, reveals a remembered significant event which remained within the family oral history for several generations.

A REVOLUTIONARY WAR SOLDIER

James Ramsey (the younger) was born and reared in the North River Settlement of of Augusta Co., VA, and became the first member of the family to known to have entered military service. He was the youngest son of James and Margaret Ramsey, and was but seven years of age when his father died in 1760. When James reached the age of military obligation, sixteen in 1769, his brother, William, had removed to Mecklenburg Co., NC, with wife, Nancy, and her brother, John Boyd, settling on the waters of Long Creek and the Gum Branch. James served from his home in the Augusta Co., VA, militia and later he would enlist in the service of the Virginia Continental Line as a soldier in Armand's Corps.

Prior to Virginia's adoption of their first State Constitution the Virginia Convention in 1775 passed an ordinance to raise two regiments, by organising the local militia with the field officers being appointed by the Convention. Virginia was divided into military districts and the militia designated as minute-men, with the counties of Augusta, Albemarle, Amherst and Buckingham being constituted as one district.[48] Each district raised a battalion of 500 men divided into ten companies of fifty, ranging from age 16 to 50, who were mustered four days a month except for the winter months of December, January and February, and being required to train twice a year for 12 days.[49] Every man was required to 'furnish himself with a good rifle if to be had, otherwise with a tomahawk, common fire-lock, bayonet, pouch, or cartouch box,[50] and three charges of powder and ball.'[51] As far as can be determined these regiments never mustered together for any engagements; and seven additional regiments were raised in December of 1775.[52] Each soldier was allowed, out of his pay, 'a hunting shirt, pair of leggings, and binding for his hat ... Pay of colonels was 17s. 6d. per day; captains. 6s. and privates, 1s. 4d.'[53]

James Ramsey's Revolutionary War pension and bounty land applications reveal that he entered the militia service as a private serving under Maj. Greg Hamilton for 3 months as a drafted soldier. The militia rendezvoused at the Albermarle Barracks, Albermarle Co., VA, and Gen. Campbell took command of the detachment. During this campaign, James was detached to maintain the horses and the personal gear of Maj. Hamilton, former commander of Augusta County troops. From Albermarle Barracks they marched to Richmond and to Petersburg. Near Bacon's Bridge they were involved in one skirmish and several American soldiers were killed. After three months service, James was discharged by Maj. Gen. Hamilton.

After remaining home about a week, James entered the service for three months as a substitute for Benjamin Smith, a son of Col. Abraham Smith of Augusta Co., VA. They rendezvoused at Richmond and marched to the Burnt Ordinary, where the American 12th were encamped, and who had shot several British sentinels at the British camp near Richmond. After the conclusion of this service, James returned home for about a week, when he volunteered for a three month tour under Capt. George Houston. Col. Bird took command of the corps, and they marched to Hampshire County, VA, to pursue and suppress the Tories. They came to the residence of John Claypole, the 'Earl of the Tories', and captured a Tory by the name of Ballew.

During this campaign the Tories surrendered their arms and promised to desist from further hostilities – a promise that would not be kept. Later in the war, after Cornwallis entered Virginia, the Hampshire Co. Tories raised the British standard on Lost River, and the militia from Berkeley, Shenandoah and Frederick Counties were mustered to suppress an insurrection led by Claypole and John Brake.[54] Claypole was arrested and released on bail, and John Brake was punished by the army, who took up free quarters for a day or two at his distillery and cowpens.[55]

In his seventy-fifth year, James Ramsey filed his petition from Rutherford Co., TN, for a pension based on his service as a private in the Continental Army, having served under the command of Col. Armand of the Dragoon line. Armand's Legion, as it came to be known, was organised at Boston in 1778, under the command of Col. Charles Armand Tuffin, who, having resigned from the French army, came to America in 1776 in order to revive his military career.[56] Armand's Legion participated in the following engagements: New York 1778, New York 1779, Defence of the Carolinas and Yorktown.[57] In 1780, Armond's Legion was sent south, to absorb the remaining troops of Pulaski, who was killed in Savannah; and, afterward removing to Virginia, to become an element of the Southern Department consisting of five companies.[58] On 1 January 1781, Armand's Legion consolidated with Capt. Bedkin's Troop of Light Horse, and reorganised as the 1st Partisan Corps consisting of three mounted and three dismounted troops; they were relieved on 11 March 1783 from the Southern Department and assigned to the Middle Department; and on 25 November 1783, they were disbanded at York, PA.[59]

James Ramsey filed for his Revolutionary War pension as a resident of Rutherford Co., TN, to obtain the benefits of the Act of Congress passed 15 May 1828, for the surviving officers and soldiers of the Army. Under the 1828 act, James was entitled to the pay of a Dragoon in the Continental Line.[60] The following is taken from James Ramsey's Revolutionary War pension claim.

REVOLUTIONARY CLAIMS

Under the act, entitled 'An act for the relief of certain surviving

Officers and Soldiers of the Army of the Revolution,' approved 13th May, 1828.

TREASURY DEPARTMENT

7 Feb. 1829

Your claim, under the abovementioned act, having been examined, you are found to be entitled to the pay of a Dragoon in the Continental Line. The amount which may be due, accordingly, will be remitted to you by the Treasurer of the United States.

(Signed) Sam'l Southard

ACTING SECRETARY

(notations: same ink and handwriting)

'James Ramsey of Rutherford Co., Tenn'.
'Care of Wm Brady, Esq. Murfreesboro, Tenn.'

CONCLUSIONS

As Ulster-Scot emigrants to America James and Margaret Ramsey established a new ancestral home in the wilderness settlement of Augusta County, Virginia, having left the familiar surroundings and the only home they had known in Ireland. They would not live to witness the harvest of their labour with their adopted country, but through their wilderness farmstead they planted the seeds of a new beginning and a new way of life for their descendants. Their story represents only one of the many thousands of Ulster emigrants who came to pre-revolutionary war America. Like an unrecognised but important thread woven and blended into the fabric of American society, these Ulster weavers, farmers, labourers, merchants and ministers have continued to make an important productive and lasting contribution through their descendants within the make-up of the multi-layered garment of American culture.

NOTES

1 Patrick Griffin, *The People with No Name* (Princeton University Press, 2000), 159.

2 R.J. Dickson, *Ulster Emigration to Colonial America 1718–75* (Routledge & Kegan Paul, 1966, reprint, Belfast: Ulster Historical Foundation, 1996), 52 and Joseph A. Waddell, *Annals of Augusta County, Virginia, From 1726 to 1871* (C.J. Carrier Company, 1979), 14.

3 Patrick Griffin, *The People with No Name* (Princeton University Press, 2000), 159.

4 Augusta Co., VA Deed Record Book 7:351–352.

5 Joseph A. Waddell, *Annals of Augusta County, Virginia From 1726 to 1871* (C.J. Carrier Company, Harrisonburg, Virginia, 1979), 150–152. See also *Augusta Co., Va., Early Settlers , Importations 1739–40* by Mrs. W.W. King, (NGSQ, Vol. XXV, June, 1937, No. 2), 47.

6 James Ramsey pension file, no. S46506, *Revolutionary Claims*, 7 February 1829, (National Archives).

7 *Ibid.* Also Joseph A. Waddell, *Annals of Augusta County, Virginia From 1726 to 1871* (C.J. Carrier Company, Harrisonburg, Virginia, 1979), 150–152.

8 *Ibid.*, 151.

9 Augusta Co., VA Will Record Book 2:426–427.

10 '20th November 1761: Allowance to Widow Ramsey and four children, objects of Charity.' Lyman Chalkley, *Chronicles of the Scotch-Irish Settlement in Virginia: Extracted From The Original Court Records Of Augusta County 1745 to 1800*, 3 vols. (Baltimore, MD, reprint: Genealogical Publishing Co. Inc., 1989), 2:448. The original Parish Book is not accessible for copying due to its' poor condition.

11 Family records of John Wesley Ramsey (1840–1901), and his daughter, Lula Virginia (Ramsey) McGee, found in possession of Richard E. Davis of Trenton, TN, 1976.

12 Rutherford Co., TN Deed Record Book U: 522–533, Register of Deeds, Murfreesboro, TN.
'This Indenture made this third day of October in the year of our Lord one Thousand eight hundred and thirty one Between William B. Ramsey of the County of Rutherford and State of Tennessee of the of the one part and Robert Overall, Nace Overall, Abraham Overall, Richard Floyd &William Ramsey Senior, Trustees in Trust for the use & purpose herein after mentioned ... being part of a Hundred Acres conveyed by William Ramsey Senior to John McKee & by him to John Davis and by him to William B. Ramsey ... that they shall erect and build or cause to be built or erected thereon a house or place of worship for the use of the members of The Methodist Episcopal Church in the United States of America ...' Among those witnesses listed as present was Wm. Ramsey, Sr, who was referred to as 'Old Ramsey'.

13 Augusta Co., VA Deed Record Book 14:42, Augusta Co., VA Court House, Clerk of the Court, Staunton, VA – 12 November 1767, 'William Ramsey and Agnis his wife ... and heir ... to his Father James Ramsey ... To Margaret Ramsey ...' Note: Nancy is the Scottish nickname for Agnes, and thereafter she used the popular name Nancy as her legal name.

14 Family Records of John Wesley Ramsey (1840–1901).

15 *Ibid.*

16 Lyman Chalkley, *Chronicles of the Scotch-Irish Settlement in Virginia: Extracted From The Original Court Records Of Augusta County 1745 to 1800*, 3 vols, (Baltimore, MD, reprint: Genealogical Publishing Co., Inc., 1989), 2:448.

17 Rutherford Co., TN Record Book 2:239, County Clerk, Murfreesboro, TN. David Rogers left his will 6 January 1813, in which he 'ordains my wife Peggy and my brother-in-law, William Ramsey as my sole executors...'

18 James Ramsey pension file, no. S46506, *Revolutionary Claims*, 7 February 1829, (National Archives)

19 *Ibid.*

20 Augusta Co., VA Will Record Book 3:6–7.

21 *Ibid.*

22 Shalloon is a lightweight twilled fabric or wool or worsted, used chiefly for linings of coats and uniforms. *Webster's Third New International Dictionary, 3 vols.* (Merriam-Webster, Inc., 1981), 3:2086.

23 Augusta Co., VA Will Record Book 3:6–7.

24 *Material Culture: an Opportunity to Study the Blending of Ethnic Traditions* by Kathleen Curtis Wilson, (The Journal of Scotch-Irish Studies, Vol. 1, Summer 2001, No. 2), 66.

25 H. Tyler Blethen and Curtis W. Wood, Jr., *From Ulster to Carolina* (North Carolina Department of Cultural Resources Division of Archives and History, Revised Ed., 1998), 66.

26 *Ibid.*, 12.

27 A colter shear is the farmer's prize possession. It is the sharp disc or other cutting tool attached to the beam of the plow. *Webster's Third New International Dictionary,* 3 vols. (Merriam-Webster, Inc., 1981), 1:450.

28 The harness of a draft animal. *Ibid.*, 3:2326.

29 H. Tyler Blethen and Curtis W. Wood, Jr., *From Ulster to Carolina* (North Carolina Department of Cultural Resources Division of Archives and History, Revised Ed., 1998), 45.

30 *Ibid.*, 59.

31 *Ibid.*, 45.

32 *Muley Cows & Brock Faced Ewes: Delving into the Ulster Roots of the Augusta County Estray Books,1775–1840* by Nancy Sorrells, (The Journal of Scotch-Irish Studies, Vol. 1, Summer 2001, No.2), 62.

33 *Ibid.*, 57.

34 Wayland F. Dunaway, *The Scotch-Irish of Colonial Pennsylvania* (1944; reprint, Baltimore: Genealogical Publishing Co., Inc., 1992), 169.

35 *Ibid.*, 188.

36 *Ibid.*, 185–6.

37 Abstracted from a copy of the original deed, maintaining the wording and spelling of the court official who created the document.

38 Augusta Co., VA Deed Record Book 14:42–47, Clerk of the Court, Staunton, VA.

39 Dower is 'the legal right or interest the wife acquires by marriage in the real estate of her husband.' James A. Ballentine, *Ballentine's Law Dictionary with pronunciations*, Edited by William S. Anderson, (The Lawyers Co-operative Publishing Company, Rochester, NY, 1969), 374.

40 There were relatively few marriages recorded for the early Scotch-Irish settlers of Augusta Co., VA. Not withstanding the high license fee for many families, the English Crown prohibited Presbyterian ministers from the north of Ireland from celebrating any of the sacraments. At common law the only requirement was for the couple to publish (post) their banns (intent) for three successive Sundays.

41 Anson Co., NC Deed Record Book 5:299–300. '31 Mar. 1759, James Anderson & wf Margaret, to Robert Boyd of same, Weaver, for £27 … 393 A on Long Cr … granted to Anderson 17 May 1754.' Brent H. Holcomb, abstractor, *Anson County North Carolina Deed Abstracts, 1749–95, Abstracts of Wills & Estates, 1749–95* (Genealogical Publishing Co., Inc., reprint 1979), 92.

42 Augusta Co., VA Deed Record Book 21:546. '8 May 1776, John Boyd, formerly of Augusta County to Joseph Douglass, tract patented to Robert Boyd 20 Sept. 1768, and vested in John as son and right heir of Robert on head of Fisher's Creek, a branch of North River of Shanando.' Lyman Chalkley, *Chronicles of the Scotch-Irish Settlement in Virginia: Extracted From The Original Court Records Of Augusta County 1745 to 1800*, 3 vols. (Baltimore, MD, reprint: Genealogical Publishing Co., Inc., 1989), 3:305.

43 Robert W. Ramsey, *Carolina Cradle, Settlement of the Northwest Carolina Frontier, 1747–62* (The University of North Carolina Press, 1964), 196–197. Fort Dobbs was built by Gov. Dobbs (north of Long Creek), about 27 miles West of Salisbury in Anson Co., NC, for the protection of these isolated settlers. Gov. Dobbs had a vested interest in several of these families, whom he brought from his lands in County Antrim, Ireland. *Ibid.*, 194.

44 Rutherford Co. TN Court Minute Book O:316, Register of Deeds, Murfreesboro, TN.

45 Rockingham Co. VA Burnt Deed Book 5: 198–199, Recorded from 'Original Deed' under the act of Assembly approved November 18th 1884, Rockingham Co., VA Court House, Register of Deeds, Harrisonburg, VA

46 Augusta Co., VA Deed Record Book 11:616, Clerk of the Court, Staunton, VA.

47 Lyman Chalkley, *Chronicles of the Scotch-Irish Settlement in Virginia: Extracted From The Original Court Records of Augusta County, Virginia 1745 to 1800*, 3 vols. (Baltimore, MD, reprint: Genealogical Publishing Co., Inc., 1989), 2: 448.

48 Joseph A. Waddell, *Annals of Augusta County, Virginia From 1726–71* (C.J. Carrier Company, Harrisonburg, Virginia, 1979), 244. Taken from *Hening's Statutes at Large.*

49 *Ibid.*

50 A gun cartridge having a paperboard case. *Webster's Third New International Dictionary,* 3 vols. (Merriam-Webster, Inc., 1981), 1:344.

51 Waddell, *Annals of Augusta County, Virginia From 1726–81, 244.*

52 *Ibid.,* 245.

53 *Ibid.,* 246.

54 *Ibid.,* 295.

55 *Ibid.* James Ramsey's militia service taken from his pension file no. S46506, (National Archives).

56 Colonial National Park Service, American Unit Lineages and Yorktown Biographies, online http://www.nps.gov/colo/Ythanout/American%20Unit%Lineages/ArmandsCorps.htm, downloaded 31 August 2002.

57 *Ibid.*

58 Colonial Park Service, American Unit Lineages, online http://www.nps.gov/colo/Ythanout/American %20Unit%20Lineages/ArmandsCorps.htm, download 31 August 2002. See Also James Ramsey's declaration of May, 1832, *Revolutionary War Rejected Bounty Land Claims,* Microfilm #12, Virginia State Archives.
    '… He (James Ramsey) being duly sworn saith that he was born and raised in Augusta County about three miles from Millers Ironworks Va that after he arrived to manhood … he enlisted in Armands Corp in the War of the Revolution and faithfaully served to the close of the War. He further says that he has never received at any time a wararant from Virginia for his service as a soldier … neither has he ever assigned or transferred his right to any person.' Notes: Bounty land claim was rejected due to receiving a pension under the Act of 15 May 1828. Miller's Ironwork's was located on Mossey Creek in Augusta Co., VA three miles S.SE of the Ramsey's homestead on the North River, between Mossey Creek and Beaver Creek. As a young man James Ramsey would have been very familiar with Miller's Ironworks, whose owners, Henry Miller (the 'iron man') and Mark Bird, entered into a partnership in 1774 as ironmasters to build necessary forges, furnace and mills. See Lyman Chalkley, *Chronicles of the Scotch-Irish Settlements in Virginia: Extracted From The Original Court Records of Augusta County, Virginia 1745 to 1800,* 3 vols. (Baltimore, MD, reprint: Genealogical Publishing Co., Inc., 1989), 3:553

59 *Ibid.* For biography of Armand in the Revolution see http://xenophongroup.com/mcjoynt/volunt.htm

60 Val D. Greenwood, *The Researcher's Guide to American Genealogy,* 3rd edition (Baltimore: Genealogical Publishing Co., Inc., 2000), 557–558. See also James Ramsey's pension file No. S46506, *Revolutionary Claims* (National Archives).

From McCorry to Curry
The Evolution of a Surname

PAUL RICHMOND

M Y CURRY ANCESTORS had their roots in a townland called Gloonan, just outside historic Gracehill village, near Ballymena in County Antrim. My interest in family history was nurtured by my grandfather, Edmond Curry, who died in June 1998 not long after he had given me some details about his parents and grandparents. However, the information I had on the family was still scant, and it took a number of years of research before I could build up a more detailed picture of the family and their story. The process was hampered by the family's constant migration throughout County Antrim during the nineteenth century and also by their frequent adoption of different variants of the surname. The 'Curry' surname was the end product of a long process of gradual modification as, from the 1830s until the early 1900s, it had evolved from 'McCorry' to 'McCurry' to 'Curry' and to make it even more complicated some members of the family later deliberately adopted the 'Currie' spelling. Furthermore, registrars and census enumerators had frequently recorded the surname incorrectly as 'Corry', or even 'Corrie'. This created a great obstacle for the inexperienced family historian, but it was eventually overcome by determination and a lot of luck.

Armed with the information which my grandfather had told me I made a trip to the General Register Office in Belfast. I had earlier found a copy of the death certificate of my great-great-grandfather, David Curry, amongst my grandfather's papers and therefore knew that

David had been 88 at the time of his death in 1961. He had lived in Belfast for many years and it seemed logical, though obviously not certain, that he would have been born in the city. Luckily only one reference in the birth indexes seemed to match his approximate birth year, and the certificate told me that David had been born on 2 January 1873 at 9 Aberdeen Street, which was located off Bower's Hill on the Shankill Road: a street which had previously been known as Hobson's Row. David was the son of David Curry, a servant, and Margaret Hunter. I also easily found the birth of David Curry junior's wife-to-be – Elizabeth Brown – but this is where the straightforwardness of my search ended. There was absolutely no trace of David Curry senior in the marriage indexes and extensive searches proved futile. The Belfast directories of 1877 and 1880 did indeed mention 'David Corry, groom' and 'David Currie, stableman', respectively, still living in Aberdeen Street, but after 1880 no trace of him could be found in the directories; this naturally prevented me from finding the Currys in the 1901 census. For a few years very little progress was made with the early roots of the Curry family tree, and I instead concentrated on researching David Curry Junior's life, aided by the information given to me by my grandfather before his death.

David had enlisted in the Royal Irish Rifles on 10 November 1890, at the young age of 17, and he went on to have a lengthy and distinguished career with the regiment lasting almost thirty years until he was honourably discharged in 1917 suffering from shellshock, having attained the rank of sergeant major. After enlisting, the young David was stationed in Fermoy, Co. Cork, but travelled home to Belfast to marry Elizabeth Brown on 5 January 1893 at Donegall Pass Presbyterian Church. Their marriage certificate states that the fathers of the bride and groom were William Brown, labourer, and David Curry, caretaker.

After their marriage David Curry Jnr and Elizabeth Brown settled in Belfast for a number of years where two of their eight children were born: Margaret in 1893, and my great-grandfather, James, in 1896. David was quite probably absent from his young family for long periods of time, as I believe he was stationed in Brighton and Aldershot between 1894 and 1896. About 1897 the Currys packed up their belongings and left Belfast with the 1st Royal Irish Rifles, bound for Ladysmith in South Africa. The family lived here for a number of years during which the Boer War loomed threateningly on the horizon, finally breaking out on 11 October 1899. The Currys' third child, William Henry Curry, was born in Ladysmith in 1899. In the same year, on 2 November, the famous siege of Ladysmith commenced. Elizabeth and her young children had clearly left the settlement before the siege began, as William Henry Curry is recorded as having been baptised in Calcutta in the same year, 1899 (the siege at Ladysmith did not end until 28 February 1900). During 1899 the 1st Royal Irish Rifles had removed to Dum Dum and Calcutta in the Indian state of Bengal (both now located in West Bengal). The frightening reports of the siege of Ladysmith which reached India would no doubt have caused David and, more especially, his young wife to have been thankful not to have still been stationed there when it began.

However, it was shortly after their arrival in India that their eldest child, Margaret Curry, who was only five-years-old, died from diphtheria. David, who was a corporal by this stage, had been away on an overland march and returned to find that his daughter was dead and buried (due to the heat the dead had to be buried within hours); David is said to have been devastated and took the news very badly. He was later stationed at the garrison in Meerut, near Delhi, during 1904 and 1905. Meerut is infamous for having been at the very epicentre of the Indian Mutiny of 1857. It was whilst living in Meerut that another of David and Elizabeth's young children died. David Curry, who was just 1 year old, died there in 1904.

The family remained in India for many years during which time David was regularly promoted, ultimately being offered the rank of sergeant major which, incidentally, he declined as he apparently preferred the rank of sergeant (he seems to have later accepted this promotion since in 1915 he is recorded as a sergeant major). It seems that accepting promotions in the Army in the nineteenth and early twentieth centuries could often cost the recipient a lot of money and this may have influenced David's decision at the time. David and Elizabeth's eight children were as follows.

Margaret Curry, born 1893 in Belfast, died at Dum Dum, Bengal, India, aged 5 in 1899. Maggie died from diphtheria. My family believed that Margaret was buried in Fyzabad, but Fyzabad and Dum Dum are quite a considerable distance apart, even though they were both in the Presidency of Bengal.

James (Jim/Jimmy) Curry, born in Belfast on 18 March 1896. James was my great-grandfather and he was born at 14 Antrim Street which was a small street which ran between Wall Street and Unity Street near Carlisle Circus. The West Link motorway now runs right over the spot where Antrim Street once stood. I had much difficulty in tracing James' birth certificate because his surname is incorrectly recorded as 'Corry' on the document. David Curry was recorded as a 'soldier' on the certificate, and the birth was registered by a woman from 19 Unity Street called Mary Walsh who had been present at the birth and who must have been one of the many 'unofficial' midwives who seem to have been very common in the city during the nineteenth century. It was possibly due to Mary's unfamiliarity with the Curry family that the surname was quoted incorrectly as 'Corry' to the registrar. My grandfather often told me that James was born in Karachi, but this has now been proven to be incorrect, perhaps the child was baptised in Karachi, or spent his formative years there hence the later confusion. James later married Jane Bunting at Drew Memorial Church of Ireland in Belfast on 31 August 1914. James became an electrician (and coincidentally lived for many years in Electric Street) and died in Belfast in the 1960s; he was buried in the City Cemetery.

William Henry Curry, born in Ladysmith and baptised in Calcutta: both events occurred in 1899. William followed in his father's foot-steps and enlisted during WWI, whilst still in his teens. His mother did not want him to join the army at such a young age, but his father insisted on letting him do as he pleased. In my possession is an old brass regimental button believed to have belonged to William, which was for many years in my grandfather's possession, and which has the word 'Inniskilling' and a castle on the front. This is the ensign of the Royal Inniskilling Fusiliers, a regiment which was founded in 1689. William married Catherine Mullen and had four children; he died in 1941 aged 42.

David Curry, born in Fyzabad, India, in 1903 and died the next year in Meerut. His death is incorrectly recorded in the Army Returns of Deaths 1901–05 under 'Currie'.

John Edmund Curry (Jack), born in Calcutta, India, in 1901 and died unmarried in Belfast on 7 February 1934. He was buried in Belfast's City Cemetery.

Lily Violet Curry, born in Fyzabad, India, in 1904. Married William Wilson, and died 8 August 1992.

Margaret Muriel Curry, born at 15 Arthur Street, Newry, on 31 January 1908. Her father is described as a 'Recruiting Sergeant' on the birth certificate. Margaret later married Samuel Curry Webb in 1934, and died 30 January 1989.

Ethel Curry, born at 23 Avonbeg Street, Belfast, on 18 February 1910. Her father is recorded on the birth certificate as being a 'Sgt. Of R.I. Rifles'. Ethel married Edmond Ritchie.

The Currys returned to Ireland about the year 1906, after a decade of life spent many thousands of miles away from their family. As they left India for good David and Elizabeth's thoughts must surely have turned to the two infants they lost during their time there, as both knew they would probably never again be able to visit their two little graves.

After researching David Curry Jnr's life for a period I then decided to try and once again tackle the difficult obstacles preventing me from discovering more about his parents' lives. I began by further checking the Belfast street directories in the hope that I could find the elusive David Curry Snr, but made no progress. It was only months later when, by pure coincidence, I was looking at the information for Waring Street in one of the late nineteenth century directories, that I finally made a breakthrough. At 58 Waring Street, in one of the directories of the late 1890s, was listed: 'D. Corry, caretaker'. I felt that perhaps this could be a misspelling of 'Curry'. The name was not referenced in any of the directories' indexes, which was why it had been so difficult to find, and Waring Street seemed like an extremely unlikely place to look for David since he had previously lived in the Shankill Road area. Waring Street was a principally commercial area in the late 1800s (and had been since the eighteenth century), consisting of banks and businesses, and so it would not have immediately occurred to me to check this location. Hopeful that this was indeed my David Curry I hastily consulted the 1901 Belfast directory and was delighted to find that 'D. Corry, caretaker' was once again listed under 58, Waring Street; this meant that there was a good chance he would be recorded at this address in the 1901 census, which may provide further leads for research. No. 58 Waring Street, in 1901, was a large mid-Victorian commercial building known as 'The Ulster Chambers', and it was predominantly occupied by the shipping firm of G. Heyn & Sons – a company which still operates in Belfast today as The Heyn Group Ltd. – as well as a number of other businesses. Upon checking the 1901 census of Waring Street I discovered that it was indeed my David Curry who was living in 'The Ulster Chambers' as a live-in caretaker:

58 WARING STREET, BELFAST

David Curry	Head	Meth.	r&w	60 M.	Caretaker	b. Gracehill, Co. Ant.
Margt. Curry	Wife	Meth.	r&w	61 M.	Housewife	b. Doagh, Co. Ant.
Wm. Curry	Son	Meth.	r&w	23 U.	Ship painter	b. Belfast City.

Fortunately, the Currys stated not only the county of their birth, but also the specific village: the only example of this which I have so far encountered in the 1901 census material for Belfast. Most of the 1901 census enumerators simply recorded the county of birth. If David and Margaret had not been so specific about their birthplaces I would most likely have never been able to locate their respective 'homelands' in County Antrim.

After having finally found the Curry family in the 1901 census many of the brick walls which I had come up against during my research were swiftly removed. For example, now that I knew the birthplace of David I was able to check the Griffith's Valuation for the Gracehill/Ahoghill area to see if there were any Currys listed there. Unfortunately there were no Currys mentioned in the valuation records in the Gracehill area (which is part of Ahoghill parish). However, there was a William Carey in Gracehill village and a Henry McCurry in Gloonan townland, which is next to Gracehill. I suspected that one of these may be related to my David Curry, but it was going to be difficult to prove it.

So, the next step was to check the various volumes of Griffith's Valuation revisions (which record the changing occupiers of the land) for William Carey and Henry McCurry's properties. William Carey's land simply passed to an Alexander Lee, but the changing ownership of Henry McCurry's seven-acre farm in Gloonan townland was much more interesting. In 1893 this farm passed into the hands of a Samuel McNeill, but later – in 1904 – the tenant once again changed, this time to a 'Henry Curry'. This therefore seemed to suggest that the McCurrys of Gloonan did indeed later change their surname to 'Curry' (assuming, of course, that both Henrys were of the same family). This naturally strengthened my belief that Henry McCurry of Gloonan was, in some way, related to my David Curry of Belfast. Henry Curry bought the land outright in 1906 (i.e. he became the owner of the land and was no longer just a tenant of it). There was a house recorded on the site in the first Griffith's Valuation of about 1859, valued at just 15 shillings. I have visited the site and it appears that this small cottage, the ancestral home of my Currys, has been either demolished or integrated into a modern house. The farm was located just to the east of the Ballykennedy Road, near the junction between it and the main Ballymena to Ahoghill road.

However, although my belief that the McCurrys of Gloonan and the Currys of Belfast were kin had been reinforced by these new findings, I still needed definitive proof. This followed swiftly after when I checked the L.D.S. family history website called 'Familysearch' for McCurry information. I did a search for a Henry McCurry, hoping to find some information on the Henry McCurry of Gloonan townland, but found, to my amazement, a listing for the birth of a Henry McCurry in Belfast in 1867, the son of a David McCurry and a Margaret Hunter. I then ordered this birth certificate and it was apparent that David McCurry was indeed my great-great-great-grandfather, David Curry. Henry was born at Hobson's Row, Belfast, on 28 September 1867, which later became Aberdeen Street – the same street in which my great-great-grandfather, David Curry Jnr, had been born in 1873. Also, rough family notes given to me by a relative confirmed that David and Margaret had indeed had a son named Henry. I had finally found proof that my Curry family had earlier used the

'McCurry' form of the surname, which further strengthened the likelihood of David and Henry being related. However, I still needed to find out for certain if, and how, my David Mc/Curry was related to Henry McCurry of Gloonan.

It is interesting that the dropping of the 'Mc' part of the surname can be quite accurately dated to the 1867–73 period, since Henry was born a 'McCurry', but his younger brother David – born in 1873 – was registered as 'Curry'. It has been suggested that the family's migration to the Shankill Road from rural County Antrim may have played a role in their decision to shorten the surname. Intense rioting occurred in Belfast during 1864, 1867 and 1872, and religious discrimination was no doubt rife throughout the town during this period. This may have encouraged David and his wife to assume a more 'anglicised' version of their surname.

Once I knew that David had formerly been a McCurry, I was able to find his marriage certificate very easily. The marriage indexes were checked and the entry for David and Margaret was found within minutes; David was listed under 'McCurry', not Curry, or even Carey, Corry or Currie, as I had previously been trying. The marriage took place on 15 December 1858 at the parish church (Church of Ireland) of Donegore and Kilbride near the small village of Doagh in County Antrim, and David was described once again as a servant. The bride and groom's fathers were Andrew Hunter and Henry McCurry, both farmers. Finding this marriage certificate therefore completed the 'circle' of research if you like: it finally enabled me to establish a definite connection between my David Mc/Curry and Henry McCurry of Gloonan. All of this focused research was made possible simply because David had specified in 1901 exactly where in County Antrim he had been born, and the census enumerator had taken the time to record it. If the enumerator had simply recorded 'Co. Antrim' as David and Margaret's birthplaces on the 1901 census there would have been very little chance of ever being able to confidently identify the correct Mc/Currys or Hunters in such a large county.

David was living at the time of his marriage in Holestone townland, just outside Doagh village. I strongly suspect that he may have been employed at Holestone House, the ancestral home of the landed

Owens family (most of whom are buried in Old Rashee Graveyard out-side Ballyclare) which was the only 'Big House' located in that town-land. David may obviously have simply been a farm 'servant' somewhere in the townland, but the use of the very deliberate word 'servant' on his marriage certificate seems to suggest that it is more like-ly that he was a domestic servant of some sort. After moving to Belfast in the 1860s David seems to have worked frequently with horses (he was described in the Belfast directories as, variously, a 'hostler', 'groom' and 'stableman') and so it is very possible that he was employed in a similar capacity in Holestone.

David's young wife, Margaret Hunter, was from the townland of Ballyhamage in Doagh – which neighbours Holestone townland – and came from quite a respectable farming family. This respectability had come about principally due to the misfortunes of the Chichester fam-ily earlier in the nineteenth century. As the Ordnance Survey Memoirs record:

> An important event, to which many may attribute their present inde-pendent circumstances, occurred about the year 1824, when, in con-sequence of the very embarrassed circumstances of their landlord (the Marquis of Donegall), who, to relieve his difficulties, granted leases in perpetuity at a mere nominal rent to such of his tenants as could pur-chase. This had for some time been foreseen by the tenantry, almost all of whom availed themselves of the opportunity. Many, by living fru-gally, were enabled of themselves to pay the necessary fine.

There were a number of Hunter families living in Ballyhamage, no doubt all related in some way. Many of the Ballyhamage Hunters are buried in Doagh Graveyard, and Andrew is quite probably amongst them, but his final resting place does not seem to be marked. Andrew's wife was quite probably Margaret Gray, and they had at least three of their children – Margaret, Maria and Andrew – baptised at the Ballyclare Circuit of the Methodist Church.

After their marriage in 1858 David and Margaret had the following seven children.

> Andrew McCurry, born *circa* 1859. Andrew strangely seemed to con-sciously adopt the 'Currie' spelling of the surname later in life, even

though all of his siblings used 'Curry'. He was a tenter and lived for many years on Broadway, Belfast, where he died in May 1917 aged 55. He was probably born in rural County Antrim before his parents migrated to Belfast. He married Margaret Alice Maher and had a number of children, including Frederick Currie, Hetty Ann Currie and Marion Ada Currie.

Henry McCurry, born 28 September 1867 at Hobson's Row, Belfast. He later adopted the 'Curry' spelling and became a baker. Henry married Margaret Young and later lived in the Woodvale area, and died in Belfast's Royal Victoria Hospital in 1927. His son, also named Henry Curry, emigrated to Australia sometime during the 1910s or 1920s. His other children included Agnes, Margaret, David, Eliza and Ellen Curry. Ellen married Robert Douglas.

David Curry Jnr, born 2 January 1873 at 9 Aberdeen Street, Shankill Road. He lived for many years on West Circular Road, Belfast. Died 3 March 1961 aged 88.

William Curry, born *circa* 1877.

Margaret Hunter Curry, born *circa* 1878, married Alfred E. Hatch in Belfast in 1898. Died in 1956 and is buried in Knockbreda Cemetery.

David and Margaret evidently had a sixth child who was alive in 1911 (they stated that they had six children living at the time the 1911 census was compiled), but I have no knowledge of him/her.

There was also a seventh child who was 'born alive' but who was deceased by the time that the 1911 census was compiled. Again, I have no knowledge of him/her.

After successfully proving that David Curry and Henry McCurry were father and son, my attention turned to the church records of the Gracehill and Ahoghill areas. It soon transpired that the McCurrys had been members of the historic Gracehill Moravian Church located in Gracehill village. The records for this congregation are very detailed throughout the nineteenth century, although the baptismal records from a number of years appear to be missing. It was whilst consulting the records of this church that it became very apparent that the Curry surname was not simply the result of one 'mutation', but two. Henry McCurry of Gloonan is repeatedly recorded in the Gracehill records as 'Henry McCorry', suggesting that the family had used this variant of the surname during the early 1800s, before adopting 'McCurry'. A total of three baptismal entries relating to the children of Henry McCurry of Gloonan, and his wife Mary, were found, although the couple had at least five children in total.

Esther McCurry, born *circa* 1833, probably in Gloonan townland. She acted as a witness at her brother David's wedding in 1858, and later married William Munce at Gracehill Moravian Church in 1864, by which time she was using the 'Curry' surname. They had one daughter that I know of, also called Esther. Esther Munce Snr died on 9 January 1923 at 14 Avondale Street, Belfast, aged 90 years, and was buried at Gracehill.

Mary Jane 'McCorry', born 4 July 1838 at Gloonan. She was baptised at Gracehill on 10 September 1838, and is recorded in the baptismal register as the daughter of Henry and Mary 'McCorry'. The witnesses to the baptism were James Titterington and Isabella Thompson.

David McCurry, my great-great-great-grandfather, born about 1839/1840 almost definitely in Gloonan townland. I cannot find his baptism in the records of Gracehill Moravian, as the baptismal records for a number of years in the 1830–40 period appear to be missing. David died on 23 June 1915, at 260 Crimea Street, Belfast, aged 75.

Eliza 'McCorry', born 23 June 1841 at Gloonan, daughter of Henry and Mary 'McCorry'. Eliza was baptised 8 October 1841 at 'parents' house, Gloonan', witnessed by James McClusky, Eliza Picken and Mary Jane Picken. There is a headstone in Gracehill Moravian Graveyard which simply records '1887 Eliza Curry' which may relate to this member of the family, although the 1887 death index does not mention any Eliza Currys, or variants.

Henry 'McCorry', born at Gloonan on 18 June 1843, baptised at Gloonan on 10 October 1843, witnessed by Henry and Mary 'McCorry'. Henry Curry is buried at Gracehill Moravian Graveyard; he died 22 May 1924 aged 80 years.

I suspect that it is this Henry Curry (born 1843) who is listed as the owner of the property in Gloonan from 1904 onwards in the early twentieth-century Griffith's Valuation revisions.

Henry McCurry was the only person of that surname mentioned in Ahoghill Parish in the first Griffith's Valuation. This seems to suggest perhaps that he was not a native of Ahoghill. The surname 'McCorry' appears in Griffith's Valuation in the County Antrim parishes of: Aghagallon, Aghalee, Ballinderry, Connor, Duneane, Glenavy, Grange of Ballyscullion, Magheragall, Rasharkin and Shankill. 'McCurry' can be found – in the same source – in the parishes of: Ahoghill, Ballinderry, Ballymoney, Billy, Blaris, Camlin, Glenavy, Layd, Magheragall, Magheramesk and Shankill. Clearly, these surnames were concentrated in the Aghalee and Ballinderry areas of south Antrim in the mid nineteenth century. The 1851 census fragments which survive for the parish of Ballinderry record no fewer than 11 McCorry households and, interestingly, the name 'Henry' appears to have been a very common, and therefore perhaps traditional, Christian name within those families throughout the 1800s. Furthermore, Ballinderry Lower is the site of one of the oldest Moravian Churches in Ireland, with the Church there having been opened for worship on Christmas Day 1751. It is well documented that members of the various Moravian congregations in Ireland often moved to other Moravian settlements and, after the closure of the communal houses at Ballinderry Lower (where single sisters and single brethren lived) the occupants are believed to have been transferred to Gracehill, but unfortunately the date of this transfer is not recorded. It is quite possible that this, or subsequent, migration within the Moravian congregations resulted in the arrival of the McCorry surname in the Gracehill area. The records of the Moravian Church at Ballinderry Lower have been checked, but no mention of Henry McCorry/McCurry has yet been found.

My next task was to search the 1901 census for the Gracehill area to see if any branches of the family remained in the old homeland. There were no Currys or variants in Gloonan or Ballykennedy townlands, nor in Ahoghill or Gracehill villages. However, I did find a family of Currys who are quite possibly connected to my family, living in Galgorm townland, which is a short distance east of Gracehill:

Henry Curry	Head	49	woollen draper	M.	B. Co. Ant.
Georgina Curry	Wife	42		M.	B. Scotland
Charles Curry	Son	10	scholar		B. Co. Ant.
Clara Curry	Dau.	6			B. Co. Ant.

David Curry	Son	7 mths		B. Co. Ant.
Mary Curry	Mother	87	widow	B. Co. Ant.
Geo. Thompson	Boarder	79	retired flax spinner	widower
				B. Co. Ant.
Alfred Marshall	Boarder	19	woollen draper Unm.	B. Eng.
				(Liverpool)
Robert Christie	Boarder	19	woollen draper Unm.	B. Co. Ant.

Everyone in the Curry household was a Presbyterian apart from George Thompson who was Baptist.

Henry's stated age on the 1901 census clearly suggests that he is not the Henry 'McCorry' baptised at Gracehill in 1841, although, from personal experience, I have found that the ages recorded on this census are often greatly inaccurate. However, I know that Georgina Curry died in Ballymena district in 1940 aged 81 but my Henry Curry's death certificate of 1924 describes him as a widower, suggesting therefore that these two Henry Currys are clearly different people. The use of the names 'Henry' and 'David' though, and the family's proximity to Gracehill village, certainly seem to imply some sort of kinship with my Currys.

My great-grandfather, James Curry, grew up on the Indian subcontinent and often sang Indian rhymes and used Indian phrases and words in later life. His mother Elizabeth enjoyed life in India as servants carried out many of the laborious chores she was used to doing at home. At the outbreak of World War One David, who was by that time a quartermaster sergeant and living back in Belfast, left for the front and did not return until 1917 after being discharged with shellshock. David and Elizabeth's son, William Henry Curry, also enlisted during WWI against the wishes of his mother, but both father and son survived the carnage of the war and returned home to Belfast.

David saw action in the Boer War, the First World War and later witnessed the devastation caused by the Luftwaffe during the Belfast Blitz of 1941. The Currys were living on Belfast's West Circular Road at the time and could see the entire city lit up by the incendiaries dropped by the German planes. One night David saw a bomb fall very near to the electric works where he knew his son James was working. He left with his son-in-law to see if they could help, but his daughter begged them not to leave and asked 'What will I do if a bomb falls on the house?' David replied 'Well, if a bomb falls on the house you'll need someone to come and dig you out, won't you!' and hurried off into the bomb-ravaged city.

James Curry married Jane Bunting at Drew Memorial Church of Ireland in Belfast in 1914. They set up home in Electric Street for a number of years and later moved a short distance to Roden Street where James lived until his death, and Jane until the early 1970s. Their children were:

> David Curry, born 20 June 1915. Died 14 July 1948 at his parents' home at 52 Roden Street.
>
> Mary Bunting Curry (Maisy), born 5 June 1917. Died 12 December 1933. Maisy was interred in Belfast City Cemetery on 14th December 1933.
>
> James Curry (Jim), born 18 September 1919. Married Bridget Dempsey and had three children. James drowned aboard Princess Victoria, a passenger ferry which sank during a violent storm in the North Channel on 31 January 1953 on its way from Stranraer to Larne. The sinking claimed the lives of 135 people. Jim's cousin, Victor B. Mitchell (son of Samuel T. Mitchell and Margaret Hoey; Margaret was a half-sister of Jane Curry, née Bunting), also drowned, and it is believed that Victor's body was recovered from the water four days after the sinking by fishermen. Jim's body was never recovered. My grandfather often told me how he and his father had to travel to Donaghadee to try and find or identify his brother's body after the sinking.
>
> Stanley Curry, born 20 March 1922. Married Nell Middleton and had three children.
>
> Lily Curry, born 7 May 1924, died 14 August 2005, aged 81. Married George Convill and had four children.
>
> Samuel Albert Curry (Sammy), born 28 October 1926 at 16 Electric Street. Samuel's father is recorded as having been an electrician at the time of his birth. Married Marie Bell and had three children. Died 25 November 1999, buried in Victoria Cemetery, Carrickfergus.
>
> John Edmond Curry (Edmond), born 25 April 1929. Married Elizabeth Gibson and had two children. Died 9 June 1998, buried in Victoria Cemetery, Carrickfergus. Edmond was my grandfather.

Norman Curry, born 17 May 1931. Married Mary Armour and has two children.

George Curry, born 20 October 1938. Married Ruby Murray and has three children.

David Curry died at his home on Belfast's West Circular Road on 3 March 1961 aged 88. His bereaved widow died just two days later and both were interred in the City Cemetery in a joint ceremony.

THE FAMILY OF ELIZABETH CURRY, NÉE BROWN

Elizabeth Brown was born at 19 Glenariff Street in Belfast on 17 December 1871. This street was located near the Sandy Row area, behind Great Victoria Street, but has long since been demolished. Elizabeth's parents were William Brown, a flax preparer, and Maria Williams. William and Maria had been married in Great Victoria Street Presbyterian Church on 6 June 1871, and later had two of their daughters, Elizabeth and Rachael Eleanor, baptised in the same church. William's father – also called William – was a school master, whilst Maria's father – Thomas Williams – was a flax spinner. Maria almost certainly had a sister named Rachael Williams, who acted as a witness at her wedding in 1871. It has also been mentioned to me that Elizabeth Brown may have had a step- or half-brother named James King, as well as a reputed connection with the celebrated Rev Henry Cooke – Elizabeth is believed to have had a cousin named Elizabeth Cooke of Agnes Street, Belfast, who was in some way distantly connected to Henry.

These are the scant facts which I currently know about the Brown family, but it is important to note that it was from similarly meagre information regarding the Curry family that my subsequent, more detailed, findings about that family grew.

Researching the origins of my Curry ancestors was made possible simply by those two place-names, 'Gracehill' and 'Doagh', being recorded on the 1901 census. These two 'keys' opened up many of the doors which had previously been firmly locked, and enabled me to finally discover where David Curry and Margaret Hunter's family roots lay before their migration to Belfast. Of course, if 'D. Corry, caretaker' had not been so luckily spotted by myself in the Belfast directories, then I would never have known to check 58 Waring Street in the 1901 census and these clues would probably never have been located.

The Currys have without doubt been the most difficult branch of my family tree to research but also, for the same reason, one of the most rewarding. The main difficulty lay in the family's propensity for modifying their surname: from McCorry in the early 1800s, to McCurry in the mid 1800s and, finally, to Curry and Currie at the end of the century. The unusual frequency with which registrars and other officials misspelt the surname also naturally made tracing the Currys that bit more difficult. I have found tracing my ancestry to be an immensely rewarding experience and it has been one throughout which I have learnt as much about myself as I have about those who are long gone. As Edmund Burke once said 'People will not look forward to posterity who never look backward to their ancestors': a knowledge of those who have gone before you is a great gift and it is one which can now – for my family at least – be shared and fully enjoyed.

In memory of my Grandfather
Edmond Curry (1929–98)

Optimum Quod Primum

Friar's Bush Cemetery
History and Horror in Two Acres of Land

JAMES BARTLETT

KING WILLIAM OF ORANGE rode past it en route to the Boyne, and it is rumoured that St Patrick himself built a church here, yet today thousands of people pass by one of the oldest cemeteries in Ireland without giving it a second glance, even though they are yards from the graves of noted Belfast inhabitants, including prominent newspapermen, the inventor of the 'Belfast Bap' as well as the notorious terrain known as the 'plaguey pit'.

The 'plaguey pit' marks the resting place of hundreds of people who perished in a major cholera epidemic in 1832–33, when bodies – most of them unidentified – were burned before burial to prevent the spread of infection. It was opened again in 1847 to take more victims of the Great Famine, at which time the Belfast Board of Guardians, then striving to cope with the pressures arising from the panic-stricken influx of rural dwellers fleeing from the famine, noted: 'According to records, cholera first appeared in Belfast in 1832, when there were 2,833 victims, with 418 deaths.'[1] In 1847–8 a wave of fever and dysentery carried off 2,487 people and cholera epidemics recurred with less vengeance, in 1848, 1854 and 1866. By 1852 it was declared to be 'excessively overcrowded' and closed soon after. Now covered in exotic herbs and flowers alien to the country, the city council has the ground left to grow wild, so they can see what other mysteries – of the biological kind – the cemetery contains.

The cemetery dates back to the medieval period when it is believed to have been the site for a friary, this being the origin for the 'friar' part of the name. The 'bush' dates back to the times of the Penal Laws, introduced following the Battle of the Boyne in 1690 which saw the Protestant Ascendancy established. Among much else the practice of Catholic Mass was well-nigh forbidden, or certainly made very difficult by these punitive laws. Arising from this exclusion, secret 'Mass Stations' were created throughout Ireland where a friar, often after being smuggled across the River Lagan, could perform the ceremony. To this day, a large and twisted thorn tree – the 'Friar's Thorn' – grows on the mound where the ceremonies were carried out. There are many stories of priests crossing the Lagan to lead services for the faithful.

> In Penal times, as peasants tell,
> A friar came with book and bell
> To chant his Mass each Sabbath morn,
> Beneath Stranmillis trysting thorn
>
> *From the poem 'The Friar's Bush' by Joseph Campbell, 1905*

It was at one of these services that a friar was murdered – some say by a shot to the heart, some say by being captured and hung from the very tree he had been preaching under. 'The poor priest had no other shelter ... than was afforded by the venerable old thorn, which on one occasion did the double duty of shadowing the Mass and afterwards serving as a gallows for the poor friar', *Ulster Observer*, 1867. 'He arrived, said Mass, but just as he turned round to give the last blessing, he fell ... shot through the heart ... he was buried where he fell, and a stone erected on the spot', *Down and Connor Historical Society Journal*, 1934.

Regardless of which tale is true, the nearby 'Friar's Stone' – marked A.D. 485 – is the reputed resting place of the friar who performed one of these secret masses, although the more likely explanation for the stone is that it is the work of a Victorian antiquarian. Even in modern times, Friar's Bush has the power to scare people away; when plans were drafted to widen the busy road outside, they were swiftly quashed when it was rumoured that disturbing the 'plaguey pit' might release something other than dead spirits back into the city.

Local expert Dr Eamon Phoenix from Stranmillis University College works alongside Gerry Ward – who runs the cemetery's website (www.friarsbush.org) and actually lives in the Gothic gate lodge – to lead tours of the cemetery, talking about its connections to Belfast and the history of Ireland, as well as its famous – and not so famous – inhabitants. The local newspaper industry is well represented, most notably with the resting places of Robert and Daniel Read, founders of the *Belfast Morning News*, the first penny newspaper in Ireland that still remains – in spirit, at least – after being incorporated into the *Irish News*. Bernard Hughes, the rags-to-riches entrepreneur and inventor of the 'Belfast Bap' – a large, round, flour-covered roll – rests alongside them.

The spookier past of the cemetery is also represented on the tour – it may only be two acres in size, but its history is far bloodier than you would expect – and looks at the 'Resurrection Men', or body snatchers, of the early nineteenth century who dug up fresh graves to sell the bodies for medical research. The most famous body snatchers were Burke and Hare – both originally from Ulster – who quickly realised that it was easier and more profitable to kill victims, rather than dig up graves. By the time they were arrested in 1828, it was estimated that they had claimed 18 victims between them, though only Burke was eventually hanged, because Hare turned King's evidence against him. Even before that most famous of body-snatching cases, Friar's Bush cemetery had fallen victim to this grisly crime: in 1823, a barrel was stopped at the docks with the bodies of a middle-aged female and a child squeezed inside and packed tight with sawdust.

Resurrectionist George Stewart had already escaped, but his partner – recorded only as Feeny – was found drunk at their lodgings in Academy Street, and investigation found that the bodies were the wife and child of Mr Bell, a shoemaker from Forest Lane, who had been buried the previous Wednesday. On searching the room, a box mailed from Edinburgh and addressed to Stewart was 'found containing a large brass syringe for injecting the veins of dead bodies, also a surgeon's knife, forceps, needle &c ... and five sovereigns'.[2] Stewart and Feeny had risked the treacherous journey across the Irish Sea from Scotland, where medical schools at Edinburgh and Glasgow were starved of corpses to dissect because laws stated that cadavers could only be those of hanged criminals. The illegal trade continued until 1832, when laws were finally changed.

There are also tragic stories of servant girls from the upper-class houses around the Malone area who, petrified of scandal and illegitimacy, are thought to have thrown their babies – alive and dead – over the wall. It is no wonder that the cemetery gained a rather dark reputation. As the artist Paul Henry (1876–1958) wrote, recalling the thrall the graveyard had for him, 'Nothing on earth would have persuaded me to enter the place … it was the house of the dead'.

More recently, since Milltown Cemetery became the main Catholic burial ground in 1869, Friar's Bush has been quiet, with the only burials that are allowed are from families with established rights – rights that are frequently contested.

NOTES

1   PRONI, BG7/A Extract from the Minutes of the Belfast Board of Guardians, June 1847.
2   *Belfast News Letter*, 15 July 1823.

Further reading: Eamon Phoenix, *Two Acres of Irish History: A Study Through Time of Friar's Bush and Belfast 1570–1918*, published by the Ulster Historical Foundation.

REVIEWS

MICHAEL MONTGOMERY AND ANNE SMYTH (EDS)

A Blad O Ulster-Scotch Frae Ullans:
Ulster-Scots Culture, Language, and Literature

The Ullans Press, Belfast, 2003

ISBN 0 053035 08 5   pp 229   £8.00

The inexorable march of time clarifies the crucial turning points in the politics and culture of Northern Ireland over the last three decades. The current fate of the Belfast Agreement of 1998 demonstrates how the society at large continues to struggle with the ramifications of more significant turning points in the 1980s and early 1990s. Predominant among these was the signing of the Anglo-Irish Agreement of 1985. That historic agreement between the Dublin and London governments enabled political parties outside of Northern Ireland to present themselves to their own constituencies as disinterested arbiters of a dispute that was internal to Northern Ireland. The agreement wrong-footed the Republican movement. It was, however, an even greater threat to Unionism and was recognised as such, because it struck a damaging blow to the tightly bound connection between the state itself and the majority culture. The stage was set for a sharp cultural turn in the politics of Northern Ireland and a new urgency on the part of political parties to articulate their politics in terms of cultural defence. The Anglo-Irish agreement created a context in which political capital is derived in part from cultural strength.

Positioning itself through the Anglo-Irish agreement outside this field, declaring no strategic interest in it, the Northern Ireland Office began to treat the political conflict in terms of the pathologies of sectarian, cultural, and ethnic differences. This re-conceptualisation of the political conflict in terms of social pathologies and citizen ignorance was made manifest in the policies of the Central Community Relations Unit, created in 1987, and subsequently the Cultural Traditions Group and the Community Relations Council, and the Department of Education's 'Education for Mutual Understanding' curricula. Those involved with the actual practice of culture – in sports, literature, music, language, and the arts – have ever since received mixed, confusing, and sometimes disturbing messages. On the one hand, our political leaders never let us forget that our fortunes in the political field, at the negotiating table, are crucially dependent on the relative strength of our cultural resources. On the other hand, multiculturalist functionaries in the education system, the museums, and in arts development inform us that this same cultural integrity is but a symptom of the wider problem. Practitioners in the field of the cultural traditions are caught in these cross-hairs.

Throughout the 1990s, the Department of Education allocated a sizable portion of its financial resources devoted to EMU (£250,000 in most years) to the Arts Council of Northern Ireland through a 'Cultural Traditions Allocation', the intention of which was to raise awareness and enhance respect on the part of our two main traditions (i.e. to raise awareness and respect by each tradition of its own cultural heritage and by each tradition of the other's heritage). In recent years the allocation has been awarded almost exclusively to organisations whose focus has been almost entirely on the first of these goals, the project of strengthening independent cultural identities.

The book under review compiles and makes available to a wider readership a sample of short pieces published between 1993 and 2001 in *Ullans*, the journal of the Ulster-Scots Language Society. The work of the USLS during this period, predominantly focused on this publication, was underpinned by grant-aid from the Cultural Traditions Allocation. The USLS has been instrumental in bringing the actual historical and contemporary material evidence of the usage of the Ulster-Scots into a wider than merely academic awareness. With this volume in hand, it is possible for a reader with no previous experience of the language and its tradition to come to a deeper understanding of what the Ulster-Scots language is, the contexts of its manifestation, and its place in the wider contemporary culture of Northern Ireland. This is not merely a matter of antiquarian interest. It is, as this oft-quoted passage from the 1998 Agreement implies, a matter of citizenship:

All participants recognise the importance of respect, understanding, and tolerance in relation to linguistic diversity, including in Northern Ireland, the Irish language, Ulster-Scots, and the languages of the various ethnic communities, all of which are part of the cultural wealth of the island of Ireland.

This passage sits in the middle of perhaps the most important piece in the volume, an essay by co-editor Michael Montgomery, a linguist and Professor Emeritus of the University of South Carolina, entitled 'What is Ulster-Scots?' and published in 2001. The date of publication is significant, reflecting the controversy sparked by the Agreement's placing of Ulster-Scots in a relation of equivalence to languages that have obviously much greater linguistic and cultural difference to the majority language of English. Nationalist and Republican participants in the revival of the Irish language in Belfast were understandably suspicious of this equivalence, particularly as Unionist supporters of the Agreement came by and large from an urban and class background which had only a tenuous connection to Ulster-Scots advocacy or its wider speech community.

In the wake of this controversy, Montgomery's essay appeals to a 'serious and open minded consideration' of the existing scholarly consensus concerning Ulster-Scots: that it is a linguistic variant of Scots and worthy of the same respect and support as Scots (Montgomery puts to one side the question of whether Scots itself is a language or a dialect); that it has a distinctive character owing to its predominantly oral manifestation; that it is a phenomenon of geographically rather than ethnically defined communities; that its proximity to English, linguistically and socio-linguistically, gives it a peculiarly subaltern character; and that a speech community with a resilient heritage of nearly four centuries is now in grave danger of extinction.

The oral and subaltern characteristics of this linguistic tradition are perhaps its most significant features. Revivalists today speak of the stigma associated with the language in relation to English. From its very origins in the seventeenth century, Ulster-Scots developed in the shadow of English, or rather within a spectrum of linguistic usage that stretched from Scots to English depending upon the social circumstances. By the evidence of this volume, the material record of Ulster-

Scots appears to be saturated by power relations. English was of course the official language of plantation, colonisation, and commerce in Ulster and on the American frontier. Appropriately enough, the earliest example of Ulster-Scots included in the volume is a lease agreement of 1614 written up by a Scottish land agent of the Haberdasher's Company, one of the twelve London merchant companies charged with colonising the new county of Londonderry:

> ... I the said Sir Robert promissis that David Cunningham and his foirsaids shall haif sufficient peit and turff yeirlie in the nixt adjacent moss thairto with ane sufficient way for carting thame to thair houssis As also gif it salhappin me the said Sir Robert and my forsaids to obtene ane Laice of the theithis of these Landis the said Sir Robert and my foirsaids promissis faithfullie that the said David his foirsaids shall haife ane sufficient richt thairoff of the cheapest rent that only other my friends sall haiff possessours of these landis . . .

The editors claim that this language is much different than that of leases written by English planters at the same time, but the differences are necessarily minimal. The text of the lease agreement had to and did correspond to the grammar and legal constructions of English-language examples from the period. The document merely concedes liberally to spellings that reflect Scottish pronunciation. The document is perfectly understandable to anyone familiar with English legal usage of the time.

Another interesting piece contributed by Montgomery discusses the work of David Bruce, born in Scotland around 1760, reared in Londonderry, and who published poetry under the pseudonym 'The Scots-Irishman' in western Pennsylvania in the 1790s. Montgomery focuses on Bruce's poem 'To Whiskey', a plea to his audience of fiercely independent Scots-Irish private whiskey distillers to submit to the Federal tax on home-distilled whiskey:

> Then foul befa' the ungrateful deil
> That would begrudge the pay right weel,
> For a' the blessings that ye yiel.
>   In sic a store;
> I'd nae turn round upo' my heel
>   For saxpence more.

It was an appeal in the vernacular tongue to the rule of law of the English speaking legislators and excise men of Philadelphia and Washington. Many of the pre-twentieth century examples of written Ulster-Scots in the volume – and here one thinks of the Victorian columnists such as John Weir, owner of the *Ballymony Observer*, or W.G. Lyttle of the *Newtownards Chronicle* – have this tactical quality, written by literate English speakers for the entertainment or edification of their bi-lingual audience.

With regard to Bruce's plea for Scots-Irish conformism, Montgomery writes (p. 114): 'though not written in pure or deep Ulster-Scots, there is much of the language in "To Whiskey"'. The last third of the book is a chronologically arranged sample of written Ulster-Scots that culminates in the near-contemporary poetry and fiction of James Fenton. As the reader moves through this material, he cannot help but wonder what 'pure or deep Ulster-Scots' might be. Indeed the most striking characteristic of this assemblage of the historical record of Ulster-Scots up to the 1990s is its accessibility to the English reader. It is only in the last decade that the English-speaking reader feels that one is reading another language altogether. Here is a passage from James Fenton's *The Flow* (p. 201):

> An yersel, a gral o a weefla, kilt wheelin tae him. For wheelin ower what grun wuz a wexer, an copin on the wunnin grun wuz knakky enugh: brek them, an a' ye'd hae at the hinther en wud be a bing o clods an a lock o coom—as a rair frae the bink wud aply mine ye.

It may be that the existence of 'pure, deep, Ulster-Scots' lies not so much in the historical record, nor in the historical actuality of a speech community for which the record is a partial reflection, but in the future production of writers for whom purity and difference are important aesthetic values. Such writers will find much to work with in the last pages of this volume.

The lease agreement of 1614 implies the existence of a large speech community among the new tenant farmers of the Ulster plantation. Likewise, Bruce's 'To Whiskey' implies the existence of such a speech community on the eighteenth century Pennsylvania frontier. What sort of a speech community does contemporary deep Ulster-Scots writing imply? Perhaps, in the spirit of the avant-garde, this writing gestures to a community that will exist only after a yet-to-come revival of Ulster-Scots. In the meantime, however, it is of symbolic importance in the wider field of culture in contemporary Northern Ireland. In their very opacity and accentuated difference from both English and contemporary spoken Ulster-Scots, these recent poems and short stories take on a commodity character, gaining their exchange value not so much from their actual form or content but from their exotic position in a cultural field in which the value of linguistic diversity and narrowly prescribed cultural identities are ascending.

The question of identity has less to do with the linguistic question 'What is Ulster-Scots?' and more to do with the social question 'Who are the Ulster-Scots?' The latter question has taken precedence over the former for two reasons. First, it was recognised almost immediately after the Agreement was signed that an effective cultural politics based on the idea of Ulster-Scots would require a movement that is larger and more urban than that of actual Ulster-Scots speakers. Second, the material reality of Ulster-Scots being geographic, not ethnic or cultural, Ulster-Scots speech is in itself an insufficient marker of cultural identity. Together, these two problems explain how language use becomes only one in a series of markers of the signifier 'Ulster-Scots,' and why the sterile debate over linguistic status was quickly surpassed by the more pressing question of Ulster-Scots cultural practices.

It is the burden of the first third of the book to establish some of these non-linguistic markers, and it is here that the material is thinnest and weakest. Here the reader finds for the most part anecdotal accounts of, for example, a tartan pattern of Ulster origin, pipe bands, place names, country dancing and square dancing, needlework, curling, and golf. The material concerning music and dance is particularly disappointing, though one piece by Philip Robinson and Will McEvoy on old-time square dancing collects some interesting evidence of dancing practice in north-east Ulster found in the Ordnance Survey Memoirs of the 1830s and in the poetry of Robert Huddleston of Moneyreagh, County Down, a generation later. The authors conclude by lamenting the lack of evidence of the exact dances and tunes used 150 years ago. What about today? The volume is rather unforthcoming about the contemporary scene. For example, a piece co-authored by Mrs Jeannie Parkes, a leading expert and teacher of the traditional dances of County Down, and Jackie Dunnan, that district's most highly regarded fiddler, addresses 'La Russe', one of the 'old figger dances' of the area. 'La Russe' is unique because, unlike most of the old sets, it has only two figures rather than the usual five or six. The article, however, gives us only the first half of the dance, and though co-authored by a fiddle player gives no information about what tunes one properly uses for accompaniment.

Scrappy though the evidence may be, this opening cultural section of the volume nevertheless provides enough material for the construction of an Ulster-Scots historical identity. Identity, after all, works by way of a series of magical steps. First, we gather together from the historical record a cluster of effective properties (Ulster-Scots speech, golf, square dancing, piping) and say this set of properties is called Ulster-Scots culture. Any one of these properties is insufficient; the ellipsis is crucial because it is the series itself, not its individual elements, that defines. Next we turn around and point to subjects and call them Ulster-Scots *because* they are (Ulster-Scots speakers, golfers, square dancers, pipers) What was an ephemeral idea, the series of characteristics in itself, is given a social body. In the next magical twist Ulster-Scots becomes that motivating ground of identity, something that is in us more than we are: We are (Ulster-Scots speakers, golfers, square dancers, pipers) *because* we are Ulster-Scots. Finally, that ground of identity is recognised *as other by one's other.*

This last step is the most difficult to achieve for the Ulster-Scots movement. One problem is that the precipitous and apparently irreversible decline since the early 1970s in the self-identification by Ulster Protestants with all things Irish has not been balanced by a corresponding decline in the self-identification by those who see themselves as Irish with things Scottish. On the contrary, recognition and celebration by Irish people of Scottish-Irish connections in traditional culture is as strong as ever. This puts the Ulster Scot proponent of traditional culture in a difficult position. Robinson and McEvoy note in their piece on square dancing: 'The term "old-time square dance" is preferred as a name to distinguish it from the Irish "set dance" tradition. Although there are some similarities between the Irish set dances and the old time square dances, the practitioners of the latter are adamant that these are not the same thing' (p. 28). To practitioners of 'Irish' set dances, however, adamancy alone may not convince. The problem is that, from Burns' nights to pipe bands, dance tunes to needlework, Irish identity has long been too inclusive of Scottish influences, and Scottish music and literature too deeply penetrated by Irish influences, to permit Ulster-Scots culture to differentiate itself meaningfully.

The predicament of Ulster-Scots culture is a manifestation of the fragility and perhaps even exhaustion of the politics of cultural difference in Northern Ireland. The work of the Ulster-Scots Language Society continues, and one looks forward to the evolution of writing in Ulster-Scots and to future volumes. One hopes that, in time, the creative potential of the language can blossom in a context that has surpassed the narrow and constraining conceptions of culture that prevail in Northern Ireland today.

MARTIN DOWLING

EILEEN M. MURPHY AND WILLIAM J. ROULSTON (EDS)
Fermanagh:
History & Society
Geography Publications, Dublin, 2004
ISBN 0 906602 52 1   pp 714   £42.50

The partition of Ireland has served to emphasise the unique character of the county of Fermanagh. To both Unionists and
Nationalists it represents the south-western bastion of the Ulster
Plantation project that continues to irritate the body politic of the Irish
Republic. Its geographical location and configuration isolate it from
the remainder of the Six Counties. As Cruickshank and McHugh
pointed out in *Land use in Northern Ireland* (1963), edited by Leslie
Symons, 'Fermanagh is the exception among the six counties in its
physical structure, its climatic regime, its pattern of land utilisation and
in its economic history.'(p. 234). This publication vastly increases the
scope of the history of Fermanagh from prehistoric times and chal-
lenges us to come to terms with evidence that is becoming more readily available. Perhaps Elizabeth Crooke will extend her study in this
volume of 'The antiquarian in nineteenth century County Fermanagh'
to assess and publicise the work of the museums, libraries, institutions,
universities, and government agencies that are engaged in the study of
Fermanagh history and society in the twenty-first century?

This attractive and well-produced volume, featuring many fine plates
and illustrations, is very welcome on many counts. In the past
Fermanagh was the only Ulster county that did not sire a *Statistical
Survey* in the series of publications promoted by the Royal Dublin
Society in the early years of the nineteenth century. Thirty years later
the project to publish parish memoirs under the aegis of the Ordnance
Survey produced little of substance beyond the basis of a good memoir
for the county town, Enniskillen and John O'Donovan's letters. Indeed
Fermanagh had to wait until the second half of the twentieth century
for its historians. In 1969 Peadar Livingstone from the Clogher
Historical Society published *The Fermanagh Story* and in 1993 Paddy

J. Duffy with the support of the same society produced *Landscapes of South Ulster: a parish atlas of the diocese of Clogher*. Jack Johnston, represented in this volume by a study of the three towns of Magherastephana barony (Brookeborough, Maguiresbridge and Lisnaskea) has inspired much good work throughout the county while Johnny Cunningham has written and published his own research.

Fermanagh is famous for its great estates and we are fortunate that great quantities of their archives have been deposited and processed in the Public Record Office of Northern Ireland. The PRONI website contains excellent essays on the contents and significance of these collections prepared under the supervision of Anthony Malcomson. His report on the Erne estate in this volume should encourage scholars to read others on the Belmore, Brookborough, Ely, Enniskillen, Armstrong of Lisgoole and Porter of Bellisle estates. In this volume, too, Robert J. Hunter has drawn from research in progress to examine the career of Sir William Cole, a soldier who rose through the ranks to become an influential planter and the creator of the county town of Enniskillen. W.A. (Bill) Maguire has explored the world of a branch of the Gaelic Maguire family that had ruled Fermanagh before the Plantation. One of the editors, William Roulston, has investigated the spate of building in the early eighteenth century of castles, churches and country houses since contemporary local historians viewed their builders as creators of a new world. Of especial interest is the corpus of work produced by the fine Strabane surveyor, William Starrat, who surveyed the Archdale estate of Manor Hassat (1716), another Archdale estate in Clanawley (1721), the Brooke estate of Colebrooke (1722 & 1736), the Belmore estate at Castle Coole (1723), and the Erne estates at Crom and Lifford (1719–22). These surveys deserve both a detailed analysis and subsequent publication.

It is a pity that the volume does not contain a study of the history of the Fermanagh grand jury which provided the effective government in the county for three centuries. About 1740 a contemporary observer claimed that its members had created the road network that linked Enniskillen with Sligo and Ballyshannon, Omagh and Clogher, Newtownbutler and Belturbet, and stimulated the cattle trade from Connacht to eastern Ulster. And yet there is no evidence about the existence of a grand jury map of the county! Gabriel Montgomery's map of Lough Erne proved an inadequate substitute. We need to res-urrect the individuals who organised Fermanagh and who answered for its peace and prosperity to the judges on their twice yearly circuits. How long did they retain the political initiative and by what stages was it transferred to other power groups such as the poor law guardians? This volume contains valuable original primary studies both on poli-tics and religion by Margaret Crawford, Myrtle Hill, Frank Thompson, Brian Barton, Eamon Phoenix and Oliver Rafferty. Each of these top-ics deserves such analysis in depth and detailed explanation of the find-ings. The subsequent step will be to study the interaction between them because they were always responding to each other as well as to external forces. How and why did change occur?

The editors of this volume were fortunate to secure contributions from Jonathan Bell and George Chambers on the nature of farming in Fermanagh. Bell interprets a wide range of sources, including the Ordnance Survey Memoirs and field notes collected for the Ulster Folk and Transport Museum, to explain the changing farming methods. This essay reflects the great value of an institution such as the UFTM in developing an ongoing dialogue with the people of the province to help them comprehend the significance of changes in society. To his study 'The rise and fall of an indigenous industry: milk processing in County Fermanagh from the seventeenth century until the present day', George Chambers has brought not only the knowledge that he gained as head of the Milk Marketing Board of Northern Ireland but also his enthusiasm for local history. He has proved an excellent chair-man of the Ulster Historical Foundation in promoting our overseas links. In this context we are all well aware of the role played by the Centre for Migration Studies based at the Ulster American Folk Park. Paddy Fitzgerald's essay explaining and illustrating the changing char-acter of emigration from Fermanagh to many parts of the world, is a most impressive contribution to the literature. This reader was sur-prised to find that for him it pointed up contrasts with the experiences of the Royal Inniskilling Fusiliers whose brief history Willie Parke had sketched out before his death.

All the volumes in the 'History & Society' series of county histories have contained reports on the progress of archaeological research and studies of language and culture. The School of Archaeology and Palaeology in the Queen's University in Belfast has provided two important studies for this volume. Eileen Murphy and Colm Donnelly review the history of archaeological research in 'Prehistoric Fermanagh' while Thom Kerr and Finbar McCormick survey early secular settlement in the county by analysing the location of ringforts or raths. Helen Lanigan Wood, the curator of Fermanagh Museum, has taken this opportunity to update her pioneer work on 'Early stone figures in Fermanagh'. These figures will continue to intrigue future generations. So too will 'The place-names of Fermanagh' which Kay Muhr explains in the latest stage of her campaign to help us to appreciate their significance. In 'Medieval Fermanagh' Katharine Simms continues her campaign to teach us about the Gaelic world that collapsed with the Flight of the Earls in 1607.

Lindsay Proudfoot and Dianne Hall have reopened for discussion the nature of Irish colonialism in their study of the career of the fourth Earl of Belmore. Patrick Maume argues for a reconsideration of the qualities and achievements of Shan Bullock, Fermanagh's most prominent writer. And Patricia Lysaght has drawn on the Irish Folklore Collection held in University College Dublin to discuss 'Death customs and beliefs of Fermanagh'. The provision of 'A select bibliography' by Enniskillen librarians, Margaret Kane and Marianna Maguire, rounds off the volume except for Margaret Gallagher's brief essay about the pleasure of living in her traditional cottage at Mullylusty.

W.H. CRAWFORD

JONATHAN BARDON

A History of Ulster

New Updated Edition

The Blackstaff Press, Belfast, 2005

ISBN 0 85640 764 X pp xxvi & 913 £15.99

The publication of Jonathan Bardon's *A History of Ulster* in 1992 was a landmark in Irish historical studies and in local publishing. A substantial work in every sense, weighing over three pounds in its paperback format and running to almost 400,000 words, it was hailed by Professor Marianne Elliott as 'the fullest, fairest and most professional history ever written of this disputed part of Ireland'. Other historians were quick to endorse this opinion and praise Bardon's meticulous scholarship and phenomenal industry. The book had an instant and well deserved success and it has since been reprinted several times. Now Blacktstaff Press have brought out a 'new updated edition' with a different, but equally striking, cover – the 'Flight of the Earls' replacing the 'Battle of Ballynahinch'. This is not, however, as might be thought, a revised edition. The only change to the text is the addition by the author of a new Introduction which brings his narrative of events as far as 2001.

This is a history so generous in its detail that it qualifies as a work of reference, indispensable for confirming those half-remembered facts of Ulster history you need to have at two o'clock in the morning when the libraries are shut. What was the 'Break of Dromore'? What was the exact sequence of events at Dolly's Brae? What were the names of the *Titanic*'s sister ships? Who was the Prime Minister of Northern Ireland between Craigavon and Brookeborough? (Dr Bardon's earlier *History of Belfast* was equally rich in recondite but interesting information.) Did you know, for instance, that Belfast's first municipal airport was on the Malone Road? (If you said Nutt's Corner, you lose five points). This is incidental. Bardon has a more serious intention than producing a manual for quiz-masters. He set out to write the first well-researched and comprehensive history of Northern Ireland as a separate entity. It is a notable contribution to historical studies if only because an earlier generation of Irish historians, whether nationalist or unionist, seemed to fight shy of putting the seal of history on partition.

Inevitably, therefore, a considerable proportion of space is devoted to politics, and quite recent politics at that. Writing against the background of the Troubles post-1969, Bardon feels obliged to find room for almost every terrorist incident and mention every politician and activist by name. This is the risk in 'contemporary history' and it makes updating tricky. It is not part of the historian's task to augment the ten o'clock news. Time is needed to distinguish the significant from the inconsequential. Bardon is too good an historian not to see the trap, even if he cannot altogether avoid it. 'Historians are frequently tempted', he writes, 'to analyse recent events with a view to predicting future developments but is is a hazardous undertaking'. This is sound advice, for by and large the chattering classes subscribe to the 'whig interpretation of history', the assumption that things are always getting better and that the story is of a steady march towards reform and democracy. Bardon concedes that 'the burden of history' may still be with us for decades to come. History itself is modest and makes no predictions. Like Ol' Man River it says nothing and just keeps rolling along.

A.T.Q. STEWART

GEOFFREY LEWIS
Carson
The Man Who Divided Ireland
Hambledon and London, London, 2005
ISBN 1 85285 454 5 pp 288 £19.99

The title of Geoffrey Lewis' new biography of Edward Carson captures the lasting legacy of the man as the architect of the partition of Ireland. Without the prestige which Carson's leadership lent to Ulster Unionism in Britain in the run up to World War One, it is by no means certain that James Craig and his supporters would have succeeded in blocking Home Rule for all Ireland.

Yet the 1933 statue of Carson at Stormont is to a large extent a monument to the Dublin lawyer's ultimate failure rather than his political success. For, as Lewis shows in this volume, Carson's overriding aim in entering politics was to preserve the union of Britain and Ireland. 'The union is my guiding star,' he declared early in his career. Partition in 1920 involved the abandonment of his 'own people' in the south and west. His bitterness welled up after the Treaty of December 1921 when he turned on his former Tory allies, accusing them of having used him and Ireland as pawns in the 'game that was to get the Conservative Party into power'.

Lewis, a lawyer and biographer of leading British legal figures, has produced an interesting life of Carson, the quintessential Irish Unionist and powerful advocate. Yet, while he draws heavily on the private papers of Lady Londonderry and the Conservative prime minister, Bonar Law, he does not add greatly to our knowledge of Carson, the man and politician. The broad outline of the Unionist leader's political evolution and public career have already been well delineated by such distinguished historians as Professor Alvin Jackson and Dr A.T.Q. Stewart.

Carson's background lay solidly in the Anglo-Irish upper class. His father was a Dublin architect of Scottish ancestry but it was from his mother, Isabella Lambert of Castle Lambert, Co. Galway, that the young Edward inherited his unflinching support for the landed ascendancy in Ireland. This alignment with Irish landlordism at a time when Gladstone's 1881 Land Act was tackling the age-old problem of peasant ownership led one Nationalist to observe of Carson: 'He has no country, only a caste.'

However, the Home Ruler Tim Healy was probably closer to the truth when he wrote that, while Carson was a Unionist, 'he was never un-Irish'. As Lewis states, Carson's political views were 'founded on the sanctity of the union between Great Britain and Ireland'. He told his aristocratic patroness, Lady Londonderry in the 1890s that he could accept no compromise on this fundamental issue. Ironically, a cousin of Carson's was Mary Butler, a strong Irish Nationalist who invented the name Sinn Fein for Arthur Griffith's separatist party.

The point is well made that while Carson's most famous association was with the northern Unionists, this period spanned little more than a decade (1910–21), while all his associations – birth, education and ancestry – placed him as a member of the Anglo-Irish Protestant minority. Leaving Trinity College, where he was a contemporary of Oscar Wilde, Carson qualified as a barrister, practising on the Leinster Circuit. He was to make his name as a fearless Crown Prosecutor during the Land War of the 1880s, prosecuting Land Leaguers and Nationalist MPs alike and was present during the fatal affray in Mitchelstown in 1887 in which two men were shot by police. His career flourished under the patronage of the Tory Chief Secretary, Arthur Balfour. By 1892, at the age of thirty-eight, he had become both MP for Trinity College and Solicitor General for Ireland in the Conservative administration. His profile continued to rise and by 1905, following the Liberal landslide, the 'lawyer with the Dublin accent' had become one of the ruling elite of the Conservative Party while his legal standing at the English Bar was reflected in earnings of twenty thousand pounds a year.

It was not until the Third Home Rule crisis in 1911 that Carson accepted the leadership of the small group of Irish Unionist MPs at Westminster. The invitation came from the shrewd but lacklustre James Craig who realised the need for a charismatic leader who could command respect at Westminster. From the outset Carson's aim was to use 'Ulster' to 'kill the Home Rule Act stone dead'. His strategy was outlined in a key letter to the Tory leader and fanatical Ulster Unionist sympathiser, Bonar Law in 1911 in which he suggested that if the Protestant North was excluded from Home Rule, John Redmond (the Nationalist leader) would reject the Bill and Home Rule would be destroyed.

It was a naïve view which allowed Carson for a few more years to feel that he was defending the rights of the Protestant minority in the south – 'his own people'. Yet, by supporting partition – albeit as a 'wrecking device' during 1912–14 – Carson was rapidly moving to accept it in principle. By 1913 he had become, in a sense, 'a prisoner' of Ulster Unionism, forced to win the best deal he could for his northern clients.

Lewis traces Carson's journey on the road to partition from the 'county option scheme' of 1914 – rejected by him 'as a sentence of death but a stay of execution for six years' – to the portentous Lloyd George partition scheme of June 1916 and the 1920 Government of Ireland Act.

Like previous historians, Lewis examines Carson's flirtation with treason and criminality in the raising of the UVF and the illegal gun running at Larne in 1913. But while others have argued that in Carson 'the lawyer was at odds with the rebel', Lewis believes that the Unionist icon had no misgivings about his involvement in these events. However, Alvin Jackson has shown that Carson was much more bellicose in public than in private and consistently counselled moderation behind the scenes. Indeed, as Lewis admits, he was prone to bouts of depression and hypochondria as his regular self-pitying letters confirm.

In this context, Carson was quick to support Lloyd George's 1916 proposals for six county partition in the wake of the Easter Rising. The 'Welsh Wizard' was undoubtedly duplicitous in his dealings with the Irish Nationalists at the time but Redmond and Joe Devlin were convinced that direct rule from Westminster would be preferable to northern nationalists than the rule of an 'Orange parliament' in Belfast.

Lewis is at his best in detailing the political intrigue surrounding the 1916 Home Rule negotiations and the role of the selfish southern Unionists in the British Cabinet in undermining Carson. Amazingly, Lansdowne and Long – as senior Tory figures with Anglo-Irish backgrounds – damaged Carson's authority by 'telling his Ulster people to throw Carson over'. Carson's authority never quite recovered from this damaging blow from his allies.

The Dublin lawyer was to play a crucial role, in concert with Lloyd George and Bonar Law, in the overthrow of the indecisive Asquith in the midst of the war in December 1916. Carson became a member of the War Cabinet but proved himself a poor administrator, too uncritical of his admirals and advisers.

His affective abandonment of southern Protestants was undoubtedly the key factor in Carson's decision to switch from Trinity College to 'a slum constituency in Belfast' in the landmark general election of 1918. The ageing politician was already being eclipsed by his deputy, James Craig, a man who had no qualms about partition. Carson stepped down from the Ulster Unionist leadership in February 1921, enjoining his northern supporters to treat the nationalist minority fairly and 'to try to win all that is best amongst those who have opposed us in the past'. Sadly, his words were to fall on deaf ears. Lewis stresses Carson's broader vision in contrast to Craig's narrow sectarianism.

Appointed a law lord in 1921, Carson's outburst during the Treaty debates at Westminster revealed his total sense of disillusionment with the Tory Party in which he had once been a major player. It was in truth the swan song of an Irish Unionist whose tradition was facing permanent defeat.

Lewis has produced a rounded profile of Carson, the Irish Unionist, British minister and effective advocate. The book ends with his elevation to the House of Lords in 1922. The author does not dwell on the disillusionment which darkened Carson's last years but he quotes Carson's remark to Blanche Dugdale (Asquith's niece) in 1928 as he surveyed the emergence of two Irish states: 'Rather a republic than this humbug.' Carson's state funeral in Belfast in 1935 – stage managed by Craig – was supremely ironic in view of Carson's essential all-Ireland Unionism and ambivalence about his political legacy.

EAMON PHOENIX

CAPTAIN JACK WHITE

Misfit
A Revolutionary Life

Livewire Publications, Dublin, 2005

ISBN 1 905225 20 2   pp 259   £14.99

Consider this absurd allegory. James Connolly, the famous Irish revolutionary, has been condemned to die by the British for his part
in a rebellion. He awaits his fate in Kilmainham Jail in Dublin. An
Ulster Protestant ex-military paladin decides to intercede. He rushes to
Wales and calls upon the miners to walk out on strike, in support of
saving Connolly, believing that's the kind of pressure the British would
heed. To develop an even more intriguing yarn, make our hero the son
of the most decorated Irish soldier in all of British military history.
Together, this unlikely duo – the soldier and the rebel – try and save
Ireland from its tempestuous future. Truth may indeed be often
stranger than fiction. The story of George and Jack White, gallant sons
of Ulster, is a striking case in point.

This review considers the autobiography of Captain Jack White,
which has recently been re-released by Livewire Publications in a
paperback version of the 1930 original, *Misfit: A Revolutionary Life*.
The cover claims that Captain Jack White 'came paradoxically from
Protestant Aristocracy stock.' This is far from the case: in fact, it is the
relatively common origins of the Whites that add to their mystique.
The primogenitor of the clan was Fulke White, who became
Presbyterian minister of Broughshane, County Antrim, three miles
from Ballymena *c.* 1687 and served there until his death in 1716. He
built the family home, 'Whitehall', there that was little more than 'a
glorified farmhouse' and acquired some 180 acres of land. His two sons
followed in their father's chosen profession.

Generations later, young George White (now Episcopalian) did not
fare so well at the local school, so he was packed off to boarding school
in the Isle of Man and from there on to Sandhurst. Promotion in the
British army was slow. At the age of 44 he was sent to Afghanistan. On

one sortie, outnumbered eight to one, his exhausted men were resigned to their fate. Major White grabbed a rifle and alone charged the enemy, setting his focus on their leader. His impromptu action caught them by surprise. With his reinvigorated men surging in behind him and its leader dead, the startled enemy was routed. For this action, White received the Victoria Cross. Thereafter promotion came more easily.

Aged 64, he was appointed General of Staff of the British forces in South Africa during the Boer War (1899–1902). His action in relieving the besieged town of Ladysmith, during which he again displayed uncanny powers of leadership and a brilliant military strategy, snatched victory from the jaws of defeat. Upon his return to England, George White was showered with every accolade in the British honours armoury. He was appointed Knight Grand Cross of St Michael and St George, Knight Grand Cross of the Royal Victorian Order, governor of Chelsea Hospital, promoted to Field Marshal. The Crown bestowed upon him the Order of Merit, reserved for the likes of Florence Nightingale and Queen Victoria befriended him. A large statue of White riding a fiery steed was placed at a busy intersection in Chelsea (eat your heart out, King Billy).

Within this household young Jack White was trying to find his place. Following in his father's footsteps, he joined the army and performed admirably, but never was able to meet his own lofty expectations. In his writings, he berates the prowess of his performance and scoffs at his well-earned Distinguished Service Order, awarded for action in South Africa (in the same Boer War in which his father also served with such distinction). When his father was appointed Governor of Gibraltar, Jack managed to be retained as his aide-de-camp. However, by this time White felt more and more that his temperament was not well suited to a military life. Reaching the rank of captain, he resigned.

Jack was a pensive and philosophical soul. A devout socialist, he voraciously read Tolstoy and other Russian revolutionary thinkers. However, he was opposed to the secularism of the Russian socialist struggle that broke out in the early years of the twentieth century, saying it ran counter to his unshakable Christian values. What shaped much of the rest of his life after the army was the close friendship he formed with another ex-British army activist. James Connolly, born in

Edinburgh, shared White's intuitive left-wing analysis for bettering the plight of the working man and, like White, was searching for a more wholesome role in life. In 1902 he went off to the United States where he spent the next eight years wrestling with socialist and labour problems and challenging sectarianism. Jack White chose Canada and stayed about one year around 1906. It proved a painful experience as he bounced west across the country from one menial job to another, trying to practise what he preached. The only steady stint was at a lumbering camp, before he finally succumbed to the severe Canadian winter.

In pre-First World War Dublin, workers were being organised by Jim Larkin, who encouraged them to come out on an unofficial strike for decent standards. The owners responded by locking the men out of the factories. Without any resources or means of support, their initiative was crushed. Into this quagmire came Connolly and White. White proposed the formation of a Citizens' Army, not for an uprising, but to 'put spirit' into the desperate men and to get leverage in the political arena. Men were recruited and drilled.

The most famous conflagration occurred at Butt Bridge in Dublin where White, the Citizens' Army and hungry workers were engaged in an illegal protest. The police were instructed to clear everyone off the street, which they performed with relish. Last man standing was White and his blackthorn shillelagh. In an amusing letter from jail to his wife he wrote, 'If I'd had my back against a wall, I believe I might be there yet'. He was charged with injuring four officers and an inspector.

White soon got into a dispute with the leadership of the Citizens' Army and Connolly and so moved to the Irish Volunteers, formed to counteract the UVF in Ulster. It grew to more than ten times the strength of the Citizens' Army and he was appointed leader of the Tyrone branch, with a reported 10,000 men turning out to drill. In an attempt to quickly bring order to the ranks, he advertised for Irish men with leadership skills. Among the first respondents was Eamon de Valera. However, White was eventually 'elbowed' out of the Tyrone command by Sinn Fein.

Upon the outbreak of the First World War in 1914, John Redmond, the leader of the Irish Nationalist Party at Westminster, appealed to the

Irish Volunteers to join the British cause and fight for freedom. Like the UVF in Ulster, a majority of them complied. The remainder formed a dissident group. It was this small band who were instrumental in organising the Easter Rising in Dublin in 1916. Among the leaders was James Connolly and it was White's bold effort in Wales to save his friend Jim (as he called him) that landed him with a three month jail sentence. It was more than a touch of ironic malice that must have prompted his captors to move White to a cell next to Roger Casement on the eve of Casement's execution.

In its subsequent settlement, the Government of Ireland Act in 1920 thrust home rule upon six counties of Ulster, with Unionism in control, a development that filled White with alarm. White later lamented that if only he had not left the Citizens' Army in a huff (his words), things could have been so different. He believed both he and Connolly could have 'pulled off a successful labor revolution'. In a letter to his mother he told her he was 'the only man who could weld a reliance between England and Ireland.' He cared deeply about maintaining the links between the two islands. At the time of the imminent split between Great Britain and Ireland, White lobbied the British establishment to permit and to promote an armed Irish militia. This he said would keep Ireland on board and be good for Britain.

In later years White fought against fascism in Spain and drifted in his thinking toward anarchism, seemingly identifying with ancient Gaelic ways, preferring Brehon to Anglo-Saxon law. It is the current worldwide interest in anarchism that has led to a rediscovery of some of White's scant writings on the subject. Original copies of *Misfit* are virtually impossible to find, creating the demand for its reissue for which the publishers are to be thanked. Jack White warns in *Misfit* that he has not told us everything and that the best was yet to come. Upon his death in 1946 the second volume of *Misfit* and other important documents are said to have been reviewed by his wife and/or the White family. The manuscript must have lived up to its billing, for his family immediately burned the lot. Jack White may have taken his best stories to the grave.

With the legacy of George and Jack White inextricably linked, one is left to ponder why they have been largely ignored by the people of

Ulster. This omission is not confined to the popular arena. For example, in Jonathan Bardon's otherwise excellent 900-page *History of Ulster* (reviewed elsewhere in this volume) Sir George White is not mentioned and Captain Jack White receives just six words, with his name consuming three of them! In Roy Foster's *History of Ireland from 1600–1972*, neither is mentioned. It is not at all inappropriate that, despite their diametrically opposed political tendencies, Sir George and Captain Jack White, father and son, are buried side by side in the Presbyterian graveyard in Broughshane, Co. Antrim … a pair of Ulster misfits?

WILLIAM J. McGIMPSEY

MONSIGNOR RAYMOND MURRAY
The Burning of Wildgoose Lodge
Ribbonism in Louth – Murder and the Gallows

Cumann Seanchais Ard Mhacha, Monaghan, 2005

ISBN 09511490 2 4 pp 359 n.p.

The most recent publication of that doyen of local history in the north of Ireland, Monsignor Raymond Murray, *The Burning of Wildgoose Lodge, Ribbonism in Louth. Murder and the Gallows,* is published by Cumann Seanchais Ard Mhacha/Armagh Diocesan Historical Society. No-one has been as productive in terms of publications or in terms of bringing to public light a range of historical issues, medieval, modern or indeed contemporary, than Monsignor Murray. His enthusiasm and attention to detail has ensured that *Seanchais Ard Mhacha,* the annual publication of this esteemed society, which has recently published its fiftieth edition, remains a model for others to follow.

The publication under review show all the benefits of the author's extensive research in the sources on both sides of the border over the years, to the extent that it is as much a social history of the area as it is a narrative of the outrages of the early years of the nineteenth century. The incident in the title, the firing of Wildgoose Lodge in Reaghstown, Co. Louth in the spring of 1816, very quickly became a *cause celebre* not only because it involved the activities of the Ribbonmen but also because the consequent court cases and eventual executions enshrined it in the already rich folklore and oral tradition of the county. It also featured in at least two of William Carleton's published works.

The book has the 'added value' of looking at a case study that has broader implications on issues such as law and order, social control and landlord-tenant relations in the context of the social maelstrom that characterised Irish society in the generation before the Famine. The immediate context for the event was the dramatic slump in prices for agricultural produce that followed very quickly the ending of the Napoleonic wars in 1815 and, with it, the thirty years of prosperity that Irish agriculture had enjoyed. On top of that, the cholera epidemic of 1816–18 contributed to the sense of dislocation in which grounds for social disturbances germinated.

Of particular interest to this reviewer were the documented references to sources illustrating the growth of dispensaries and their role in trying to contain the spread of the typhus epidemic. It was also gratifying to see that Harold O'Sullivan's influence on research and writing on Louth history continues unabated.

TREVOR PARKHILL

WILLIAM LAFFAN (ED)

SAMUEL CHEARNLEY
Miscelanea Structura Curiosa
with introductory essays by
Toby Bernard, Christine Casey and William Laffan
and an appendix by Peter Harbison
Churchill House Press, Tralee, 2005
ISBN 0 955902 460 9 pp 173 incl. 83 plates €85.00

This is the first publication of a series of drawings which, had they been published in the mid-1740s (as seems to have been the intention), 'would have been the first book devoted to garden buildings anywhere in Europe' (p.9). The architect who drew them, Samuel Chearnley, died in 1746 (or could his traditional date of death be an Old Style rendering of 1747?), since which time they have remained in the possession of the Earls of Rosse, the descendants of his cousin and patron, Sir Lawrence Parsons, 3rd Bart (1708–56) at Birr Castle, Co. Offaly. They are therefore a most important survival and their eventual publication an important event.

The introductory essays are well-informed and enlightening. They establish the context, historical and aesthetic, in which Chearnley worked, without taking away from the individuality, wit and whimsy of his *oeuvre*. Inevitably – or was it? – there is some overlap between and among these three contributions and a good deal of repetition. Christine Casey's piece, in particular, though in its own right excellent, seems to have been written in isolation from the other two. But this is to cavil. At least, the three contributors do not disagree and what they all have to say is first-rate. The happiest discovery of the introduction was made – not surprisingly – by the encyclopaedic Toby Bernard who shows, from the evidence of letters in the archive of the Physico-Historical Society in Armagh Public Library, that Chearnley designed the (still surviving) column on which the statue of the Duke of Cumberland used to stand in the middle of Birr. This column is therefore the only design by Chearnley which definitely was executed.

The production of the drawings is a little fuzzy, and in some plates the foxing of the papers has been so accentuated that it looks as if sooty fingers had turned the pages. All the instances of cropping are presumably to be attributed to the post-1922 re-binding of the volume (a matter referred to in the cropping of Chearnley's signature). His sometimes indistinctly reproduced comments on the drawings are transcribed at pp. 152–6, which is as well.

A word needs to be said about the personal contribution of the present Earl and Countess of Rosse to this publication. For as long as I have been associated with the archive at Birr Castle (a period of some twenty-five years) they have been ardent champions of Chearnley and have done what they could to ensure that the significance they saw in the drawings should be communicated to a wider public. In fulfilling this aspiration they have now been well served by William Laffan, Toby Barnard and Christine Casey, who bring to the task a scholarship and a lightness of touch which have been worth waiting for.

A.P.W. MALCOMSON

BILL JACKSON

Ringing True
The Bells of Trummery and Beyond
350 years of an Irish Quaker family
William Sessions Ltd, York, 2005
ISBN 1 85072 329 X pp 241 £16.00

It would be a problem for most people to locate Trummery on a map, even for those of us who live in Ulster; it is not a place well known to anyone beyond those who live in its immediate vicinity. Yet the townland of Trummery, one of eleven townlands in the parish of Magheramesk, was the spot where Archibald Bell, from Arkinholme in Dumfriesshire in Scotland settled when he came to Ulster in the 1650s. For those readers who are still wondering where it is, Trummery lies just east of the village of Moira, on the County Antrim side of the River Lagan, marked by crossroads on the main road (not the M1) to Lisburn.

Bill Jackson, whose mother was a member of the Bell family, has written a history of this family since their arrival from Scotland over 350 years ago. As the author readily admits, the Bells were not in any sense members of the nobility, nor even the gentry; rather, they were middle-class, hard-working, some becoming prosperous, Quakers. They were, in fact part of the backbone of the Ulster-Scots community who, by their labours, helped shape the Ulster we know today. Indeed, it is an interesting fact that, rather than espouse Presbyterianism, which would have been the religion of their Scottish forebears, they immediately joined the Society of Friends in their new homeland, along with many other settlers who had arrived in counties Armagh and Down, principally from the north of England.

Any researcher into Quaker history has the benefit of detailed records which have been preserved by the Society of Friends. Bill Jackson has made full use of these records, as have other members of the Bell family in earlier years: their notes and genealogies have provided the basis for this work. Indeed, the Bell family, on a worldwide scale, seems to have had considerable interest in their family history; it remained to the present author to piece it all together and bring it up to date.

The book is divided into convenient chapters, each covering a century, from the seventeenth to the twenty first; these years cover no fewer than thirteen generations. Each chapter provides the historical setting of that century as far as the family was involved: settlement, the linen industry, the cotton industry, business, emigration and the wars of the twentieth century. At the end of each chapter, there is a family-by-family listing of family members of that century, with their dates of birth, marriage and death, names of spouses and children and place of residence or Meeting to which they belonged. Every name has a figure (1, 2, 3 etc.) indicating to which generation he or she belonged. As time goes on, the necessity for this identification becomes clearer because of the repetition of the same Christian names throughout the generations. Many of these names are in bold type which indicates that the author has supplied a short biography of the individual. These biographies are in themselves of tremendous interest in that they, to coin a phrase, put flesh on the bones. Of course, many family members cross over between two centuries: in these instances, the generation identifying number helps the reader keep track of them.

From the early years of the nineteenth century, various members of the Bell family left their mark on the linen industry, at that time in transition from a cottage industry to a more fully mechanised major industry. Drawing largely on the notebooks of James A. Beck in the Public Record Office of Northern Ireland, the author gives a detailed picture of the various companies which different members of the family founded or in which they became involved, located from Belfast through Whiteabbey to Ballyclare and, most importantly, in Lurgan, close to where the original Archibald had settled in Trummery almost two centuries earlier. Brothers Thomas and Samuel founded Thomas Bell and Company of Bellevue, just north of the town, specialising in cambric. Later the family purchased a power loom factory operated by the Macoun brothers in the centre of Lurgan and renamed it The Lurgan Weaving Company Limited. This company continued trading until after World War II, although the original Thomas Bell and

Company had ceased trading in in the early 1920s.

Throughout the book, the principles and ethics of the Society of Friends are very evident: William Bell, in the early nineteenth century, as well as being involved in the temperance movement, played a prominent role in the anti-slavery movement. On the other hand, a later Bell, who became Ricardo, made his fortune in the sugar plantations in Cuba around the same period. The author's perseverance is evident in the fact that he has been in correspondence with a distinguished businessman in Venezuela, who just happened to be a keen genealogist, to supply these facts! Other members of the family pursued journalism as a sideline: a later William was instrumental in launching *The Irish Friend* in 1837 which, although short-lived, was the blueprint on which *The British Friend* was modelled.

In later years, members of the family emigrated to America where they found success in business, some acting as shipping agents for the burgeoning freight traffic across the Atlantic. They built fine houses for themselves: Bill Jackson has been in touch with the appropriate historical societies where the family is still remembered and, indeed, later generations still live. Some Bells emigrated to Australia and also to New Zealand where they now farm no less than 24,000 acres.

This book takes its place among those histories with an appeal far beyond the immediate family. Whilst the family and thumbnail sketches of the individual members remain the centrepiece of the story, that story is enriched by glimpses of the wide society in which they lived. They left their mark on that society in a variety of ways: one has received the distinction of being a Fellow of the Royal Society and the present generation in Belfast has a respected architectural practice, as well as being prominent members of the Society of Friends. The book has many photographs of earlier members of the family, individually and in groups, adding considerably to the reader's enjoyment. Bill Jackson has put us all in his debt: future generations will have cause to be grateful to him for this work, a monument to the achievement of a remarkable Ulster family.

J. FRED RANKIN

JANE MEGAW

The Sun-Dialled Meeting-Houses, Cullybackey a Short History of the Cuningham Memorial Presbyterian Church and its Predecessor

Available from the Congregational Committee

c/o 21 Dreen Road, Cullybackey, BT42 1EB

2005 173 pp £10.00 plus postage

One hundred years ago, in April 1905, Hume & Gray of Royal Avenue, Belfast held a two-day auction of Irish antiquities which had been collected by the late Revd Dr George Raphael Buick of Cullybackey, County Antrim. The Ulster Museum holds artefacts first assembled by that sometime Moderator of the Presbyterian Church in Ireland who was a son of the Revd Frederick Buick, the long-lived minister of Second (Trinity) Ahoghill congregation, and Matilda Raphael of Galgorm (see this reviewer's edition of Buick's Ahoghill, Ballymena, 1987).

On 12 February 2004, in advance of the centenary of the younger Buick's death during deputation work in Damascus on 28 April 1904, Jane Megaw saw published her affectionate account of his former congregation. A member of the Ulster Genealogical and Historical Guild (see her 'A Few Lines More' in the Subscribers' Interest List 11) she had been typically clever in her choice of main title. It refers to John Wylie's item of 1727 which was preserved in 1881, when the Cuningham family of Ardvernis replaced an earlier, altogether more plain meeting-house with 'the most impressive building in the village'. That sponsoring family, whose money came from linen, predictably receives substantial coverage, its New Zealand branch having travelled back in 2003 with the trowel which laid the foundation-stone of the Gothic edifice in 1880. But a far wider range of folk will enjoy this account which is replete with names of people in their rural places. Come of Broughshane stock, Miss Megaw had a deep appreciation of townlands, whether Ballyclosh or Ballywatermoy, Crankill or Kildowney, Dunnygarron or the Dreen.

Very well illustrated with documents, ephemeral and otherwise, and bound in a cover as insistently blue as the deepest Presbyterian carpet, this book includes the staple information about ministers, events and organisations required by the genre. But the author, who had once been a professional migrant, teaching in Cliftonville, north Belfast, has still remained an insider in the community on which she wrote. Whether in passing comment, often tantalising, amid more mundane detail or in a range of appendices about the wider social contexts of the congregation, she showed herself to be empowered by a long memory and a ready ear for lore. She had taken her place in a distinguished authorial succession, after the three Given brothers, James S. Loughridge, William Shaw and others, in what has been by far the most literary village in mid-Antrim.

Having seen her immediate project of more than a decade's gestation enthusiastically launched by the congregation on 12 February 2004, in the presence of the Moderator of that day, Miss Megaw had further authoritative work to do on local records and on her own reminiscences, especially on her clachan of Markstown. Alas, exactly one month later, she died suddenly, aged eighty-two and a lively, genealogically-inclined mind was stilled. Yet, we give thanks for what she was able to complete. Her own memorial will be much appreciated by coming generations of the Cullybackey diaspora.

EULL DUNLOP